Moving Beyond the Grammatical Syllabus

In this concise and practical book, Martel advocates for a content-based approach to foreign language curriculum design that emphasizes communicative competence, cognitive engagement, and social justice. Intended primarily for busy teachers with limited preparation time, the book includes:

- An introduction to content-based instruction and its use to date in foreign language education
- Step-by-step strategies for designing content-based unit plans, lesson plans, and assessments
- A complete curricular unit that serves as a guiding example, including nine lesson plans and a summative assessment

The book is accompanied by a website that will feature additional examples of content-based curricular materials across a range of languages and proficiency levels, available at http://cbi.middcreate.net/movingbeyond.

Jason Martel is an associate professor of TESOL/TFL at the Middlebury Institute of International Studies in Monterey, CA.

T0347474

Routledge Focus on Applied Linguistics

Making Sense of the Intercultural
Finding DeCentred Threads
Adrian Holliday and Sara Amadasi

Mobile Assisted Language Learning Across Educational Contexts
Edited by Valentina Morgana and Agnes Kukulska-Hulme

Complicity in Discourse and Practice
Jef Verschueren

Moving Beyond the Grammatical Syllabus
Practical Strategies for Content-Based Curriculum Design
Jason Martel

Contesting Grand Narratives of the Intercultural
Adrian Holliday

Sustainability of Blended Language Learning Programs
Technology Integration in English for Academic Purposes
Cynthia Nicholas Palikat and Paul Gruba

For more information about this series, please visit: https://www.routledge.com/Routledge-Focus-on-Applied-Linguistics/book-series/RFAL

Moving Beyond the Grammatical Syllabus

Practical Strategies for Content-Based Curriculum Design

Jason Martel

Routledge
Taylor & Francis Group

NEW YORK AND LONDON

First published 2022
by Routledge
605 Third Avenue, New York, NY 10158

and by Routledge
2 Park Square, Milton Park, Abingdon, Oxon, OX14 4RN

Routledge is an imprint of the Taylor & Francis Group, an informa business

© 2022 Taylor & Francis

The right of Jason Martel to be identified as author of this work has been asserted in accordance with sections 77 and 78 of the Copyright, Designs and Patents Act 1988.

All rights reserved. No part of this book may be reprinted or reproduced or utilised in any form or by any electronic, mechanical, or other means, now known or hereafter invented, including photocopying and recording, or in any information storage or retrieval system, without permission in writing from the publishers.

Trademark notice: Product or corporate names may be trademarks or registered trademarks, and are used only for identification and explanation without intent to infringe.

Library of Congress Cataloging-in-Publication Data
Names: Martel, Jason, author.
Title: Moving beyond the grammatical syllabus : practical strategies for content-based curriculum design / Jason Martel.
Description: New York, NY : Routledge, 2022. | Includes bibliographical references and index.
Identifiers: LCCN 2021045705 (print) | LCCN 2021045706 (ebook) | ISBN 9780367819163 (hardback) | ISBN 9781003017424 (ebook)
Subjects: LCSH: Language and languages—Study and teaching. | Curriculum planning. | Language arts—Correlation with content subjects.
Classification: LCC P53.295 .M38 2022 (print) | LCC P53.295 (ebook) | DDC 418.0071—dc23/eng/20211025
LC record available at https://lccn.loc.gov/2021045705
LC ebook record available at https://lccn.loc.gov/2021045706

ISBN: 978-0-367-81916-3 (hbk)
ISBN: 978-1-032-16458-8 (pbk)
ISBN: 978-1-003-01742-4 (ebk)

DOI: 10.4324/9781003017424

Typeset in Times New Roman
by codeMantra

Contents

Tables

Acknowledgments

There are many people whose kind support made this book project possible. To those who read drafts of various parts of the book, including Netta Avineri, Kristin Davin, Clarissa Eagle, Zoya Erdevig, Kate Paesani, Francis Troyan, Kristen Tuttle, and Keli Yerian: thank you for your thorough, honest, and useful feedback. To Mark Amengual and Kim Helmer: thank you for your friendship and for helping me navigate academic life as gracefully as possible. To Daniel Correia: thank you for your companionship and for holding me up through the rough moments. And finally, to my students: thank you for your patience with my pedagogical experiments and for your challenging questions, which greatly enhanced the quality of the ideas recorded in these pages.

Introduction

According to Clementi and Terrill (2013), "[a] dynamic world language curriculum forges connections between and among the other disciplines allowing learners to explore interesting questions and issues while acquiring linguistic and cultural proficiency" (p. iii). I strongly believe that one of the best ways to achieve this type of curriculum is to implement content-based instruction, also known as CBI. The goal of the book is to provide foreign language teachers[1] with concrete strategies for designing content-based curricular materials, including unit plans, lesson plans, and assessments. This goal aligns with current conceptualizations of effective foreign language teaching in the United States, which ask teachers to "create content-based lessons that integrate language, culture, and student interests around topics drawn from a variety of subject areas" (ACTFL/CAEP, 2013, p. 14).

CBI has been a longstanding passion of mine. I first learned about it as a high school French teacher in the suburbs of Boston, while doing research on the website for the Center for Advanced Research on Language Acquisition (CARLA) at the University of Minnesota. I visited this website because I wanted to learn how to make my French classes more engaging and intellectual. I was so captivated by what I learned that I decided to pursue my PhD at the University of Minnesota. I was excited to study with Diane Tedick, who states on her faculty webpage that "teaching language through content is the most effective approach to teaching second/foreign languages, and there is ample research evidence to support that conviction" (Regents of the University of Minnesota, n.d.). After completing my PhD, I was lucky to get a job at the Middlebury Institute of International Studies at Monterey, which has a rich history of content-based language education for students in fields such as international education management, international environmental policy, and nonproliferation studies (see Gillen, Gueldry, & Harmer, 2010; Shaw, 1996; Snow & Brinton, 2017). These

DOI: 10.4324/9781003017424-1

experiences have given me the opportunity not only to research CBI, but also to enact it with actual French language learners, providing a laboratory for the principles and practices I share throughout this book.

In line with my teaching experiences, the book is written principally for practicing foreign language teachers in secondary (i.e., middle and high school) and tertiary (i.e., college and university) settings. It can be used in professional learning communities (Vescio, Ross, & Adams, 2008) or as a self-study guide. The book is also designed for candidates in foreign language teacher preparation programs, provided it is used alongside comprehensive manuals such as Shrum and Glisan's (2016) *Teacher's Handbook: Contextualized Language Instruction* or Curtain and Dahlberg's (2016) *Languages and Learners: Making the Match*, which provide a basis of key pedagogical concepts that this book largely assumes of its readers. Furthermore, the book is written principally for foreign language teachers in the United States, with its grounding in frameworks like the American Council for the Teaching of Foreign Languages' (ACTFL) *World-Readiness Standards for Learning Languages* (National Standards Collaborative Board, 2015), which I refer to henceforth as "the ACTFL Standards." However, it is also relevant to foreign language teachers in other countries, such as English teachers in Japan or French teachers in Brazil, for whom the conditions of language teaching are somewhat similar. Readers whose local version of content-based language teaching is known as "content and language integrated learning" (CLIL) will also likely find the book helpful, particularly those in "Model B4" secondary programs (Coyle, Hood, & Marsh, 2010). Like Cenoz (2015), I believe that "CBI/ CLIL programmes share the same essential properties and are not pedagogically different from each other" (p. 8).

The book has four core chapters, whose contents are rooted in two key premises: (1) that thematic unit planning should occur "independent of textbooks" (Clementi & Terrill, 2013, p. 26) and (2) that content should be addressed initially when designing a thematic unit's architecture. I follow Tedick (2003), who holds that in CBI, "the linguistic elements that make up language (i.e., grammatical structures, vocabulary, etc.) emerge naturally from the content and are understood within the context of that content" (p. 10). In Chapter 1, I provide important background information about CBI and discuss how content-based planning interacts with our identities as foreign language teachers. In Chapter 2, I describe concrete strategies for designing what I call a thematic unit's "content nucleus," that is, the core content around which the unit will be built. In Chapter 3, I address ways of unpacking content and language integrated learning goals and assessment procedures. In Chapter 4, I present practical techniques for designing content and language integrated lessons that fit into the thematic architecture put into place in Chapters 2 and 3. To conclude the book, I revisit the interaction between CBI and our identities as foreign language teachers, in addition to offering parting thoughts on topics such as conceptualizing complete content-based courses and using CBI with novice-level learners. I know that many foreign language teachers are worried about using CBI with students who are at the beginning of their language learning process, so I highlight concrete strategies aimed at alleviating this concern.

Throughout the book, I share examples from my own French teaching at the Middlebury Institute of International Studies, principally from a content-based thematic unit titled "(Anti)racism in Quebec." This three-week unit was delivered to ten Intermediate Low-level students (ACTFL, 2012) during a fall 2020 course titled "Social Issues in Contemporary Quebec." It has since been revised based on personal reflections and several rounds of feedback. Due to the COVID-19 pandemic, the course was taught online, with a balance of synchronous and asynchronous elements. Students in the course were pursuing master's degrees in international policy and management (e.g., international environmental policy, international education management, and nonproliferation and terrorism studies). I designed a content-based course not only because of the Middlebury Institute's grounding in CBI, but also to help the students learn content and language that would expand their capacity as internationally focused professionals. In addition to these examples, the book contains key resources for further study and reflection questions for you to ponder either alone or in a group setting.

I truly hope this book provides you with interesting ideas, as well as concrete practices that you can start using in your teaching right away. Let's begin our adventure into CBI!

Reflection Questions

- How do you incorporate other academic disciplines into your foreign language courses?
- Have you heard of CBI? If so, what do you know about it?
- Which foreign language pedagogical manuals have you studied? What did they say about curriculum design? What did they say about content-based instruction?
- How comfortable are you with designing original curriculum?

Note

1 This book is equally applicable to those who self-identify as "world language" teachers. Although I consider the moniker "foreign language" to be imperfect, I retain it owing to its continued usage in the United States. See Graves (2008) for more sophisticated contextual labels, e.g., "target language-removed" and "target language-embedded" (p. 155).

References

ACTFL. (2012). *ACTFL proficiency guidelines 2012.* https://www.actfl.org/resources/actfl-proficiency-guidelines-2012

ACTFL/CAEP. (2013). *ACTFL/CAEP program standards for the preparation of foreign language teachers.* https://www.actfl.org/sites/default/files/caep/ACTFLCAEPStandards2013_v2015.pdf

Cenoz, J. (2015). Content-based instruction and content and language integrated learning: The same or different? *Language, Culture, and Curriculum, 28*(1), 8–24. http://dx.doi.org/10.1080/07908318.2014.1000922

Clementi, D., & Terrill, L. (2013). *The keys to planning for learning: Effective curriculum, unit, and lesson design.* ACTFL.

Coyle, D., Hood, P., & Marsh, D. (2010). *CLIL: Content and language integrated learning.* Cambridge University Press.

Curtain, H., & Dahlberg, C. (2016). *Learners and languages: Making the match: World language instruction in K–8 classrooms and beyond* (5th ed.). Pearson.

Gillen, M., Gueldry, M., & Harmer, J. (2010). The Monterey Model: An interdisciplinary platform for integrating professional core competencies. In M. Gueldry (Ed.), *How globalizing professionals deal with national languages* (pp. 101–125). The Edwin Mellen Press.

National Standards Collaborative Board. (2015). *World-readiness standards for learning languages* (4th ed.). Author.

Shaw, P. (1996). Voices for improved learning: The ethnographer as co-agent of pedagogic change. In K. M. Bailey & D. Nunan (Eds.), *Voices from the language classroom: Qualitative research in second language education* (pp. 318–337). Cambridge University Press.

Shrum, J., & Glisan, E. (2016). *Teacher's handbook: Contextualized language instruction* (5th ed.). Cengage.

Snow, M., & Brinton, D. (2017). *The content-based classroom: New perspectives on integrating language and content.* University of Michigan Press.

Regents of the University of Minnesota (n.d.). *Diane J. Tedick.* https://www.cehd.umn.edu/ci/people/tedick.html

Tedick, D. (2003). *CAPRII: Key concepts to support standards-based and content-based second language instruction* (pp. 1–13). University of Minnesota.

Vescio, V., Ross, D., & Adams, A. (2008). A review of research on the impact of professional learning communities on teaching practice and student learning. *Teaching and Teacher Education, 24*(1), 80–91. http://dx.doi.org/10.1016/j.tate.2007.01.004

1 CBI and Foreign Language Education

In this chapter, I commence our exploration of CBI with important background information. First, I define CBI. Then, I explain how it has been implemented to date in foreign language education. Next, I make the core argument of this book: that we should adopt what is called a content-driven (Met, 1998) approach to CBI in foreign language education. Finally, I discuss what planning for a content-driven approach to CBI means for our identities as foreign language teachers.

1.1 Definitions of CBI

CBI is defined as "a curricular and instructional approach in which nonlinguistic content is taught to students through the medium of a language that they are learning as a second, heritage, indigenous, or foreign language" (Tedick & Cammarata, 2012, p. S28). There's a lot to unpack in this definition. First, CBI is identified as a curricular *approach*, which is understood to represent "a vision of what education should be and the role it should play" (Tedick & Cammarata, 2010, p. 244). Second, content is qualified as "nonlinguistic," which includes information, concepts, or ideas from other school subject areas such as biology or cultural studies (Lyster, 2011), as well as "any topic, theme or non-language issue of interest or importance to…learners" (Genesee, 1994, p. 3). In this conceptualization, content does not include metalinguistic information about grammar structures. Finally, it is indicated that instruction in CBI classrooms should occur primarily in the additional (i.e., target) language.

A crucial element of CBI's effectiveness is "the concurrent and balanced teaching of both *language* and *content*" (Cammarata, Tedick, & Osborn, 2016, p. 12, emphasis in original; see also Lyster, 2017). The synergistic relationship between language and content is referred to in the CBI literature as *counterbalance* (Lyster, 2007). In counterbalanced

DOI: 10.4324/9781003017424-2

instruction, "language and content can be conceptualized as comple-
mentary options in a dynamic relation that optimizes L2 learning"
(Tedick & Lyster, 2020, p. 81). In other words, language and content
should both receive attention in the curriculum, continually propel-
ling and never stifling each other. Furthermore, counterbalanced
instruction includes both reactive and proactive elements (Tedick &
Lyster, 2020). Responding to a student's oral language error with a
recast represents an example of reactive counterbalance, whereas selecting a specific language focus "designed intentionally to highlight
connections between subject-matter content and the language needed
to engage with that content" (Tedick & Lyster, 2020, p. 82) represents
an example of proactive counterbalance. Reactive counterbalance is
primarily an instructional concern (i.e., enacted during class), whereas
proactive counterbalance is primarily a planning concern (i.e., planned
for before class). This book addresses the latter.

CBI is practiced in a broad range of contexts and "differs in terms
of factors such as educational setting, program objectives, and target population" (Snow, 2014, p. 439). In an effort to classify the different types of content-based foreign language programs, Tedick and
Cammarata (2012) designed a matrix featuring two key variables:
time and curricular focus. The time continuum of the matrix includes
high and low time-intensive poles, while the curricular focus continuum includes content- and language-driven poles. To give an example,
early total immersion programs[1] are considered to be high time-
intensive and content-driven, as students spend a significant amount
of time during the school day operating in the target language, and
subject-area content (e.g., math, social studies) is the driving curricular force. In contrast, foreign language programs (e.g., French I in a
high school or second semester German in a college) are considered to
be low time-intensive and language-driven, as students spend only a
small portion of the school day in language courses, and language is
typically the driving force for curriculum design.

1.2 CBI in Foreign Language Education

This book focuses on CBI implementation in low time-intensive
and language-driven foreign language education programs, a context I refer to henceforth as "foreign language education." I chose
this focus because CBI has not yet enjoyed widespread adoption in
foreign language education, despite reported interest starting in the
early 1980s. Dupuy's (2000) literature review on CBI includes several

studies between 1981 and 1997 under the rubric of "theme-based studies" that were carried out in foreign language courses. These studies, all of which were conducted at the tertiary level, revealed continued positive findings in the domains of language competence, subject matter learning, and self-confidence/motivation. To give two examples, Lafayette and Buscaglia (1985) found that students in an intermediate-level French course who were exposed to CBI felt more positive about the lessons they received and were more interested in continuing their French studies than students who received a traditional skills-based curriculum. Klee and Tedick (1997) found that students in an intermediate-level content-based Spanish course made significant gains on multiple measures of language learning, including a cloze task, an elicited imitation task, and vocabulary and writing tests. More recent studies of CBI at the university level (e.g., Rodgers, 2006) have also yielded positive results from a language learning perspective.

There are far fewer studies that document CBI implementation at the middle and high school levels. Those that exist revealed positive findings concerning language learning, subject matter learning, and self-confidence/motivation, like the higher education studies mentioned above. At the high school level, Cumming and Lyster (2016) studied the implementation of a content-based unit on environmental issues in a French III course. They found that students made gains in grammatical gender accuracy on immediate and delayed post-tests. At the middle school level, Pessoa et al. (2007) studied the implementation of CBI in two sixth grade Spanish classrooms. Importantly, they demonstrated that different conceptualizations of CBI can influence student learning outcomes. To elaborate, one of the teachers in the study, James, focused primarily on language form while implementing CBI, whereas the other teacher, Grace, asked her students to expand on their opinions related to content. Perhaps surprisingly, Grace's students outperformed James' in multiple language domains (e.g., vocabulary, language control) on a writing assessment, even though James more frequently focused on form during his teaching. The study's authors posited that this interesting finding may be related to discursive factors: that Grace "routinely negotiated form with her students, while James' approach to accuracy relied heavily on the direct provision of the correct form by the teacher embedded in evaluative feedback sequences" (p. 114).

Given the positive outcomes reported in these studies, it is curious to me that CBI has not become more widespread in foreign language education. I suspect this is largely due to the hegemony of language-driven commercial textbooks, which is closely associated with the limited time teachers generally have during their workdays to focus on curriculum design.

1.3 A Rationale for CBI in Foreign Language Education

Many scholars have outlined research- and theory-based rationales for implementing CBI across a range of foreign/second language contexts, including Byrnes (2005), Cammarata et al. (2016), Donato (2016), Dupuy (2000), Fitzsimmons-Doolan, Grabe, and Stoller (2017), Jourdenais and Shaw (2005), Lain (2016), Stryker and Leaver (1997), Met (1991, 1998), Tedick and Cammarata (2010, 2012), and Tedick and Wesely (2015). In this section, I build on these publications by highlighting four reasons why I consider it advantageous to foster widespread adoption of CBI in foreign language education.

First, CBI helps facilitate the development of communicative competence. According to Lyster (2007), CBI provides "the requisite motivational basis for purposeful communication" (p. 2). Planning for CBI implicates all three of the ACTFL's Communication Standards: interpersonal communication, interpretive communication, and presentational communication (National Standards Collaborative Board, 2015). The three modes of communication represent students' ability to:

- interact and negotiate meaning in spoken, signed, or written conversations to share information, reactions, feelings, and opinions (interpersonal communication);
- understand, interpret, and analyze what is heard, read, or viewed on a variety of topics (interpretive communication); and
- present information, concepts, and ideas to inform, explain, persuade, and narrate on a variety of topics using appropriate media and adapting to various audiences of listeners, readers, or viewers (presentational communication; National Standards Collaborative Board, 2015, paras. 2–4).

These modes of communication are vital to CBI because they help students access information and ideas in texts and then discuss and share what they learned with others. It is well understood that in foreign language education, communication hasn't always been front and center. Foreign language teachers have historically spent too much time focusing on analyzing language structures at the expense of cultivating students' ability to use structures to communicate meaningfully and authentically with others (Cammarata et al., 2016; Martel,

2013b; Tedick & Walker, 1994). Implementing CBI helps us to reposition knowledge about language (i.e., metalinguistic knowledge) as a tool for facilitating authentic social exchanges rather than as an end itself (Celce-Murcia, 1991; Hall, 2001; Liamkina & Ryshina-Pankova, 2012; Paesani, Allen, & Dupuy, 2016).

Second, language-driven foreign language courses have consistently yielded underwhelming outcomes. Data from the Center for Applied Second Language Studies (CASLS, 2010) revealed that the average American high schooler who studies foreign language for four years attains a proficiency level of Novice High/Intermediate Low, meaning they use primarily memorized phrases and can barely create novel utterances when attempting to communicate (see also Cammarata et al., 2016 and Martel, 2016). Similarly, Rubio and Hacking (2019) noted that "after two semesters of instruction, students in post-secondary institutions show only Novice levels of proficiency" and that "[e]ven after four semesters, proficiency does not always reach the Intermediate level" (p. 137). Inspired by the research reviewed in the previous section, I believe a content-based approach can do better, keeping in mind Hlas' (2018) Grand Challenge for foreign language education to "[i]mprove the functional proficiency of all students at a level that allows them to interact for personal and professional pursuits" (p. 4).

Third, prioritizing content provides an opportunity to systematically incorporate critical thinking into the curriculum, in line with the Modern Language Association's (MLA) support for "a broad, intellectually driven approach to teaching language and culture" (MLA Ad Hoc Committee on Foreign Languages, 2007, para. 1). I argued previously that foreign language education remains a relatively "thinking light" subject (Martel, 2016). I supported this claim with three types of evidence: (1) data from my dissertation study, in which the participant, a Spanish teacher candidate, felt pressure from her students to be an "easy" teacher (Martel, 2013a); (2) an explanation of the conservative rituals and beliefs that characterize the "deep structure" of foreign language education, such as thin/stereotypical culture teaching, that leave little room for intellectual exploration (Burke, 2011); and (3) an analysis of one state's unpacking of the ACTFL Standards, which failed to engage students in critical thinking until far into the multiyear learning sequence (Massachusetts Department of Education, 1999). CBI provides the opportunity to integrate thought-provoking content into all levels of the foreign language curriculum with an emphasis on critical thinking skills. In fact, critical thinking has long been a key feature of CBI. Met (1991) noted that "[l]anguage learning through content has the...advantage of allowing an integration with higher order thinking tasks, so that students may communicate about thoughts, not just words" (p. 282). Furthermore, Cammarata et al. (2016) articulated the following goals for a content-based approach to foreign language education:

- placing the development of critical thinking and advanced literacy skills at the forefront;
- stimulating students intellectually and cognitively through the development of higher-order thinking skills; and
- fostering students' intellectual sensitivity (pp. 9–10).

Finally, and I believe most importantly, prioritizing content provides an opportunity to systematically address issues related to social justice. As I am writing these words, so many people in the United States continue to be victimized by unjust policies and practices in a "time of ubiquitous pain" (Ennser-Kananen, 2016, p. 556). Through CBI, we can integrate content into the foreign language curriculum that relates the many forms of injustice that pervade our society and that helps students cultivate necessary critical thinking skills for working to dismantle these injustices (Martel, 2016). Thankfully, there is exciting work already underway in this domain, known as "critical CBI" (CCBI), whose goal is to "(re)locate language education as something integral to society" (Sato, Hasegawa, Kumagai, & Kamiyoshi, 2017, p. 51). A great example of CCBI is Kubota's (2012) Japanese curriculum that explored the power dynamics inherent in victim and victimizer perspectives in Japanese culture related to the events of World War II. Outside CCBI, there is a broader push to integrate social justice issues into the foreign language curriculum, as reflected in publications by Bruzos (2017), Caballero-García, (2018), Glynn and Spenader (2020), Glynn, Wesely, and Wassell (2018), Meredith, Geyer, and Wagner (2018), and Wassell, Wesely, and Glynn (2019).

1.4 A Rationale for Content-Driven CBI in Foreign Language Education

As stated above, this book focuses on content-based curriculum design in foreign language education programs, which are considered to be low time-intensive and language-driven (Tedick & Cammarata, 2012). In general, when content is integrated into such programs, it is used as context for practicing language forms, preserving an underlying grammatical syllabus—what Curtain and Dahlberg (2016) call "content-related instruction." In content-related programs, "the focus...is on language learning and the content is used as a vehicle to make that learning more engaging" (Curtain & Dahlberg, 2016, p. 54). I think a shift is in order. Following Cammarata et al. (2016), I argue that we should adopt a content-driven approach to CBI in foreign language education, which entails replacing language with content as our field's curricular "underlying organizing principle" (p. 8; see also Met, 1998). In a previous publication (Martel, 2013b), I provided three reasons for this shift. First, content-driven syllabi help us reposition language as a social tool for meaning making rather than an object to be analyzed (Tedick & Walker, 1994). Second, we know from a copious amount of research on second language acquisition that language forms are not learned in the tidy sequences reflected in grammar-driven syllabi (see Ellis & Shintani, 2014). Third, the status quo of grammar-driven curricula has produced lackluster outcomes, as explained in the previous section. To this list of reasons, Cammarata et al. (2016) add that "most traditional methods of language instruction with their overt focus on form often confuse learners about the true nature of the language learning experience, making its potential for intellectual development go unnoticed" (p. 8).

Crucially, I am not suggesting that we stop focusing on language in our courses. Rather, I am challenging us to think about content first when designing curriculum and then to use content as a guide for determining which language forms to address (Tedick, 2003). I understand that this represents a significant rupture from how foreign language curriculum has been traditionally created. However, I strongly believe it is worth the effort based on the reasons provided in this and preceding sections. As daunting as it may be, I aspire in this book to make such an approach feasible by detailing a set of practical strategies for content-driven curriculum planning, in Chapters 2 through 4. I draw inspiration from Heineke and McTighe's (2018) *Using Understanding by Design in the Culturally and Linguistically Diverse Classroom*, which blends strategies from Wiggins and McTighe's (2005) *Understanding by Design* (UbD) framework with ones that foster language development. However, the present book differs from Heineke and McTighe (2018) in that it is intended for a primary audience of foreign language teachers, who are principally language-trained, as opposed to general subject area teachers, who are principally content-trained. In light of this difference, I highlight special strategies for elaborating the content side of the planning equation—an area in which we as foreign language teachers are typically not as well versed.

1.5 CBI and Identity

Although this book features practices for designing content-driven, content-based curricular materials, it is also my intention to highlight various identities that you may or may not currently associate with yourself and your work. By identities, I mean the ways in which you see yourself as a foreign language teacher, or, in other words, the meanings you associate with yourself in your role as a foreign language teacher (see Martel, 2013a).

A lot of research has been conducted on language teacher identities, and on teacher identities within education more broadly. This research has revealed several key insights, notably that identities are fluid and dynamic (Varghese, Morgan, Johnston, & Johnson, 2005), meaning they can change over time, and that they are deeply intertwined with practice, meaning they are negotiated through the act of teaching (Kanno & Stuart, 2011; Reeves, 2018). Identity construction is a key facet of teacher learning, in addition to knowledge and skills development (Beijaard, 2019). Building on this conceptualization of learning, I have made the case along with other scholars that identity and innovation are deeply intertwined (Freeman, 2013; Martel, 2017; Trent, 2014). Indeed, if we are invested in the success of educational innovations such as CBI, we need to address identities associated with these innovations, not simply concomitant skills and knowledge. As such, I follow Reeves (2018), who holds that teacher education should involve helping teachers to "imagine alternative teacher identities" and that "[s]uch imaginative work can lead to the creation of new, different instructional practices, which are better suited to teachers' contexts and to social justice than the ingrained but perhaps ill-fitted and inequitable instructional practices in place" (p. 5).

There are many meanings you likely already associate with yourself as a foreign language teacher, specifically, and as a teacher in general. For instance, you may see yourself as a role model for your students (Martel, 2013a). In this book, I invite you to explore three specific identity positions while planning for CBI, which you may already inhabit to varying extents. First, I invite you to see yourself as an innovator (Martel, 2017). I encourage you to revel in trying new things and expanding your pedagogical repertoire, as is asked of us by standards of professional practice that highlight the importance of reflection and continued professional growth (e.g., ACTFL/CAEP, 2013; National Board for Professional Teaching Standards, 2010). Second, I invite you to see yourself as a curriculum designer (Clandinin & Connelly, 1992; Philippou, Knotovourki, & Theodorou, 2014; Rosiek & Clandinin,

2016; Tedick & Lyster, 2020; Tomlinson, 2001). I urge you to take an active role in designing activities and assessments for the courses you teach rather than unquestioningly using what is provided by your textbook (if indeed you use one). Third, I invite you to see yourself as both a content *and* language teacher, or in other words, as an *integrated* content and language teacher. Research has demonstrated that teachers in content-based settings tend to see themselves as either content *or* language teachers (e.g., Cammarata & Tedick, 2012; Tan, 2011), and I have argued that this is related in part to the curricular nature of teacher preparation programs, which tend to emphasize either language or content (Martel, 2020). In planning for CBI, I hope that you will come to see yourself as someone who is responsible for facilitating your students' learning on a broader scale than language alone.

In asking you to consider these potentially new identities, and to work toward inhabiting them, I am also inviting you to exercise your agency as a foreign language teaching professional. Agency is defined as "the capacity of people to act purposefully and reflectively on their world" (Rogers & Wetzel, 2013, p. 63; see Kayi-Aydar, 2019, for further definitions). Agency is understood to be deeply connected to social contexts, meaning that your ability to exert agency as a foreign language teacher depends in part on the conditions of your workplace. To give an example, I have recommended that you take an active role as a curriculum designer, yet you may work in a program in which you are required to cover certain textbook chapters in a specified time. If this is the case for you, I recommend that you exert agency by working with the ideas in this book and presenting a case to your administrators as to why diverging from the textbook would be beneficial for your students' learning. In offering this course of action, I am inspired by Kayi-Aydar (2015), who stated, "[w]hen [people] are able to exercise agency, they can construct the identities that they wish to construct" (p. 141).

1.6 Summary

In this chapter, I laid the groundwork for our exploration of content-based curriculum design for foreign language education. I defined CBI and reviewed accounts of implementation across multiple levels of instruction. Most importantly, I called for a content-driven approach to CBI, which involves determining the content-based aspects of curricular materials before deciding how to scaffold language. In the next chapter, I begin describing concrete strategies for designing content-driven curricular materials, starting with a focus on content.

1.7 Reflection Questions

- Which approaches in foreign language education are you familiar with?
- What role does (non-linguistic) content play in your curriculum?
- What is the relationship between language and content in your curriculum?
- How does it feel to consider content first and then language when designing curriculum?
- How are the three modes of communication reflected in your curriculum?
- What proficiency gains do your students make in your courses? How do you know this?
- How is critical thinking reflected in your curriculum?
- How is social justice reflected in your curriculum?
- What are some of the facets of your identity as a foreign language teacher?
- How much agency do you feel like you have in your teaching context? Do you feel like you can effect change?
- What excites you about CBI? What scares you?
- Based on what you've read so far, does CBI seem feasible in your teaching context?

1.8 Key Resources

- *Content-Based Foreign Language Teaching: Curriculum and Pedagogy for Developing Advanced Thinking and Literacy Skills* (Cammarata, 2016). This book includes chapters on a wide range of pertinent topics from prominent scholars in the field, with an overall emphasis on critical thinking and social justice.
- *Teaching for Success: Developing Your Teacher Identity in Today's Classroom* (Olsen, 2016). This book helps teachers understand their role identities and the various forces that bear upon their identity construction.
- "Implementing Content-Based Instruction: The CoBaLTT Framework and Resource Center" (Tedick & Cammarata, 2010). This chapter gives an overview of CBI and presents the Content-Based Language Teaching with Technology (CoBaLTT) website, which will be referenced frequently throughout this book.

Note

1 To learn more about early total immersion programs, as well as other types of immersion programs, see Fortune and Tedick (2008).

References

ACTFL/CAEP. (2013). *ACTFL/CAEP program standards for the preparation of foreign language teachers.* https://www.actfl.org/sites/default/files/caep/ACTFLCAEPStandards2013_v2015.pdf

Beijaard, D. (2019). Teacher learning as identity learning: Models, practices, and topics. *Teachers and Teaching: Theory and Practice, 25*(1), 1–6. http://dx.doi.org/10.1080/13540602.2019.1542871

Burke, B. (2011). Rituals and beliefs ingrained in world language pedagogy: Defining deep structure and conventional wisdom. *Journal of Language Teaching and Research, 2*(1), 1–12. http://dx.doi.org/10.4304/jltr.2.1.1-12

Bruzos, A. (2017). Encuentros con el español: A case study of critical service learning in the Latino community. In S. Dubreuil & S. Thorne (Eds.), *AAUSC volume 2017: Engaging the world: Social pedagogies and language learning* (pp. 37–63). Cengage.

Byrnes, H. (2005). Content-based foreign language instruction. In C. Sanz (Ed.), *Mind and context in adult second language acquisition* (pp. 282–302). Georgetown University Press.

Cammarata, L. (Ed.). (2016). *Content-based foreign language teaching: Curriculum and pedagogy for developing advanced thinking and literacy skills.* Routledge. http://dx.doi.org/10.4324/9780203850497

Cammarata, L., & Tedick, D. (2012). Balancing content and language in instruction: The experience of immersion teachers. *Modern Language Journal, 96*(2), 251–269. http://dx.doi.org/10.1111/j.1540-4781.2012.01330.x

Cammarata, L., Tedick, D., & Osborn, T. (2016). Content-based instruction and curricular reforms: Issues and goals. In L. Cammarata (Ed.), *Content-based foreign language teaching: Curriculum and pedagogy for developing advanced thinking and literacy skills* (pp. 1–21). Routledge.

Center for Applied Second Language Studies (CASLS). (2010). *What proficiency level do high school students achieve?* https://casls.uoregon.edu/wp-content/uploads/pdfs/tenquestions/TBQProficiencyResults.pdf

Celce-Murcia, M. (1991). Grammar pedagogy in second and foreign language teaching. *TESOL Quarterly, 25*, 459–480.

Caballero-García, B. (2018). Promoting social justice through 21st century skills: Thematic units in the language classroom. *Dimension, 130*, 145.

Clandinin, D., & Connelly, F. (1992). Teacher as curriculum maker. In P. W. Jackson (Ed.). *Handbook of research on curriculum* (pp. 363–401). Macmillan Publishing Company.

Cumming, J. & Lyster, R. (2016). Integrating CBI into high school foreign language classrooms. In L. Cammarata (Ed.), *Content-based foreign language teaching: Curriculum and pedagogy for developing advanced thinking and literacy skills* (pp. 77–97). Routledge.

Curtain, H., & Dahlberg, C. (2016). *Learners and languages: Making the match: World language instruction in K–8 classrooms and beyond* (5th ed.). Pearson.

Donato, R. (2016). Sociocultural theory and content-based foreign language instruction. In L. Cammarata (Ed.), *Content-based foreign language* teaching: *Curriculum and pedagogy for developing advanced thinking and literacy skills* (pp. 25–50). Routledge.

Dupuy, B. (2000). Content-based instruction: Can it help ease the transition from beginning to advanced foreign language classes? *Foreign Language Annals, 33*(2), 205–223. http://dx.doi.org/10.1111/j.1944-9720.2000.tb00913.x

Ellis, R., & Shintani, N. (2014). *Exploring language pedagogy through second language acquisition research.* Routledge. http://dx.doi.org/10.1017/S0272263102002073

Ennser-Kananen, J. (2016). A pedagogy of pain: New directions for world language education. *Modern Language Journal, 100*(2), 556–564. http://dx.doi.org/10.1111/modl.1_12337

Fitzsimmons-Doolan, S., Grabe, W., & Stoller, F. (2017), Research support for content-based instruction. In M. Snow & D. Brinton (Eds.), *The content-based classroom: New perspectives on integrating language and content* (2nd ed., pp. 21–35). University of Michigan Press.

Fortune, T., & Tedick, D. (2008). One-way, two-way and indigenous immersion: A call for cross-fertilization. In T. W. Fortune & D. J. Tedick (Eds.), *Pathways to multilingualism: Evolving perspectives on immersion education* (pp. 3–21). Multilingual Matters.

Freeman, D. (2013). Teacher thinking, learning, and identity in the process of educational change. In K. Hyland & L. C. Wong (Eds.), *Innovation and change in English language education* (pp. 139–154). Routledge.

Genesee, F. (1994). *Integrating language and content: Lessons from immersion* (Educational Practice Report No. 11). National Center for Research on Cultural Diversity and Second Language Learning.

Glynn, C. & Spenader, A. (2020). Critical content-based instruction for the transformation of world language classrooms. *L2 Journal, 12*(2), 72–93. https://doi.org/10.5070/L212246307

Glynn, C., Wesely, P., & Wassell, B. (2018). *Words and actions: Teaching languages through the lens of social justice* (2nd ed.). ACTFL.

Hall, J. (2001). *Methods for teaching foreign languages: Creating a community of learners in the classroom.* Pearson.

Heineke, A., & McTighe, J. (2018). *Using Understanding by Design in the culturally and linguistically diverse classroom.* ASCD.

Hlas, A. (2018). Grand challenges and great potential in foreign language teaching and learning. *Foreign Language Annals, 51*(1), 46–54. http://dx.doi.org/10.1111/flan.12317

Jourdenais, R., & Shaw, P. (2005). Dimensions of content-based instruction in second language education. In R. Jourdenais, & S. Springer (Eds.). *Content, tasks and projects in the language classroom: 2004 conference proceedings* (pp. 1–12). Monterey Institute of International Studies.

Kanno, Y., & Stuart, C. (2011). Learning to become a second language teacher: Identities-in-practice. *Modern Language Journal, 95*, 236–252. http://dx.doi.org/10.1111/j.1540-4781.2011.01178.x

Kayi-Aydar, H. (2015). Teacher agency, positioning, and English language learners: Voices of pre-service classroom teachers. *Teaching and Teacher Education, 45*, 94–103. http://dx.doi.org/10.1016/j.tate.2014.09.009

Kayi-Aydar, H. (2019). Language teacher agency: Major theoretical considerations, conceptualizations, and methodological choices. In H. Kayi-Aydar, X. Gao, E. Miller, M. Varghese, & G. Vitanova (Eds.), *Theorizing and analyzing language teacher agency* (pp. 10–21). Multilingual Matters.

Klee, C., & Tedick, D. (1997). The undergraduate foreign language immersion program in Spanish at the University of Minnesota. In S. Stryker & B. Leaver (Eds.), *Content-based instruction in foreign language education* (pp. 141–173). Georgetown University Press.

Kubota, R. (2012). Memories of war: Exploring victim-victimizer perspectives in critical content-based instruction in Japanese. *L2 Journal, 4,* 37–57. http://dx.doi.org/10.5070/L24110009

Lafayette, R., & Buscaglia, M. (1985). Students learn language via a civilization course—A comparison of second language classroom environments. *Studies in Second Language Acquisition, 7*(3), 323–342.

Lain, S. (2016). Content-based instruction understood in terms of connectionism and constructivism. *L2 Journal, 8*(1), 18–31. http://dx.doi.org/10.5070/L28128902

Liamkina, O., & Ryshina-Pankova, M. (2012). Grammar dilemma: Teaching grammar as a resource for making meaning. *Modern Language Journal, 92*(2), 270–289. http://dx.doi.org/10.1111/j.1540-4781.2012.01333_1.x

Lyster, R. (2007). *Learning and teaching languages through content: A counterbalanced approach.* John Benjamins. http://dx.doi.org/10.1075/lllt.18

Lyster, R. (2011). Content-based second language teaching. In E. Hinkel (Ed.), *Handbook of research in second language teaching and learning, Vol. 2* (pp. 611–630). Routledge.

Lyster, R. (2017). Language-focused instruction in content-based classrooms. In M. Snow & D. Brinton (Eds.), *The content-based classroom: New perspectives on integrating language and content* (pp. 109–123). University of Michigan Press.

Martel, J. (2013a). *Learning to teach a foreign language: A student teacher's role identity negotiation.* [Doctoral dissertation, University of Minnesota]. Proquest.

Martel, J. (2013b). Saying our final goodbyes to the grammatical syllabus: A curricular imperative. *French Review, 86*(6), 1122–1133. http://dx.doi.org/10.1353/tfr.2013.0106

Martel, J. (2016). Tapping the National Standards for thought-provoking CBI in K–16 foreign language programs. In L. Cammarata (Ed.), *Content-based foreign language teaching: Curriculum and pedagogy for developing advanced thinking and literacy skills* (pp. 101–122). Routledge.

Martel, J. (2017). Identity, innovation, and learning to teach a foreign/second language. In G. Barkhuizen (Ed.), *Reflections on language teacher identity research* (pp. 87–92). Routledge.

Martel, J. (2020). The identities of language-trained content-based teachers: An underexplored community of practice. *Teacher Learning and Professional Development, 5*(1), 37–48.

Massachusetts Department of Education. (1999). Massachusetts foreign language curriculum framework. http://www.doe.mass.edu/frameworks/foreign/1999.pdf.

Meredith, B., Geyer, M., & Wagner, M. (2018). Social justice in beginning language instruction: Interpreting fairy tales. *Dimension*, *90*, 112.

Met, M. (1991). Learning language through content: Learning content through language. *Foreign Language Annals*, *24*(4), 281–295.

Met, M. (1998). Curriculum decision-making in content-based language teaching. In J. Cenoz & F. Genesee (Eds.), *Beyond bilingualism: Multilingualism and multilingual education* (pp. 35–63). Multilingual Matters.

MLA Ad Hoc Committee on Foreign Languages. (2007). Foreign languages and higher education: New structures for a changed world. *Profession 2007*, 234–245.

National Board for Professional Teaching Standards. (2010). *World languages standards*. https://www.nbpts.org/wp-content/uploads/ECYA-WL.pdf

National Standards Collaborative Board. (2015). *World-readiness standards for learning languages* (4th ed.). Author.

Olsen, B. (2016). *Teaching for success: Developing your teacher identity in today's classroom* (2nd ed.). Routledge. https://doi.org/10.4324/9781315638621

Paesani, K., Allen, H. W., & Dupuy, B. (2016). *A multiliteracies framework for collegiate foreign language teaching*. Pearson.

Pessoa, S., Hendry, H., Donato, R., Tucker, G. R., & Lee, H. (2007). Content-based instruction in the foreign language classroom: A discourse perspective. *Foreign Language Annals*, *40*, 102–121. http://dx.doi.org/10.1111/j.1944-9720.2007.tb02856.x

Philippou, S., Knotovourki, S., & Theodorou, E. (2014). Can autonomy be imposed? Examining teacher (re)positioning during the ongoing curriculum change in Cyprus. *Journal of Curriculum Studies*, *46*(5), 611–633. http://dx.doi.org/10.1080/00220272.2013.856033

Reeves, J. (2018). Teacher identity. *The TESOL encyclopedia of English language teaching*. http://dx.doi.org/10.1002/9781118784235.eelt0268

Rodgers, D. (2006). Developing content and form: Encouraging evidence from Italian content-based instruction. *Modern Language Journal*, *90*(3), 373–386. http://dx.doi.org/10.1111/j.1540-4781.2006.00430.x

Rogers, R., & Wetzel, M. (2013). Studying agency in literacy teacher education: A layered approach to positive discourse analysis. *Critical Inquiry in Language Studies*, *10*(1), 62–92. http://dx.doi.org/10.1080/15427587.2013.753845

Rosiek, J., & Clandinin, D. (2016). Curriculum and teacher development. In D. Wyse, L. Hayward, & J. Pandya (Eds.), *The SAGE handbook of curriculum, pedagogy and assessment* (pp. 293–308). http://dx.doi.org/10.4135/9781473921405.n19

Rubio, F., & Hacking, J. (2019). Proficiency vs. performance: What do the tests show? In P. Winke & S. Gass (Eds.), *Foreign language proficiency in higher education* (pp. 137–152). Springer.

Sato, S., Hasegawa, A., Kumagai, Y., & Kamiyoshi, U. (2017). Content-based instruction (CBI) for the social future: A recommendation for critical content-based language instruction (CCBI). *L2 Journal*, *9*(3), 50–69. http://dx.doi.org/10.5070/L29334164

Snow, M. (2014). Content-based and immersion models of second/foreign language teaching. In M. Celce-Murcia, D. Brinton, & M. Snow (Eds.), *Teaching English as a second or foreign language* (4th ed., pp. 438–454). National Geographic Learning/Heinle Cengage Learning.

Stryker, S., & Leaver, B. (1997). *Content-based instruction: From theory to practice.* Georgetown University Press.

Tan, M. (2011). Mathematics and science teachers' beliefs and practices regarding the teaching of language in content learning. *Language Teaching Research, 15*(3), 325–342. http://dx.doi.org/10.1177/1362168811401153

Tedick, D. (2003). *CAPRII: Key concepts to support standards-based and content-based second language instruction* (pp. 1–13). University of Minnesota.

Tedick, D., & Cammarata, L. (2010). Implementing content-based instruction: The CoBaLTT framework and resource center. In J. Davis (Ed.), *World language teacher education* (pp. 243–273). Information Age Publishing.

Tedick, D., & Cammarata, L. (2012). Content and language integration in K–12 contexts: Student outcomes, teacher practices, and stakeholder perspectives. *Foreign Language Annals, 45*(S1), S28–S53. http://dx.doi.org/10.1111/j.1944-9720.2012.01178.x

Tedick, D., & Lyster, R. (2020). *Scaffolding language development in immersion and dual language classrooms.* Routledge. http://dx.doi.org/10.4324/9780429428319

Tedick, D., & Walker, C. (1994). Second language teacher education: The problems that plague us. *The Modern Language Journal, 78*, 300–312.

Tedick, D., & Wesely, P. M. (2015). A review of research on content-based foreign/second language education in US K–12 contexts. *Language, Culture, and Curriculum, 28*(1), 25–40. http://dx.doi.org/10.1080/07908318.2014.1000923

Tomlinson, B. (2001). Materials development. In R. Carter & D. Nunan (Eds.), *The Cambridge guide to teaching English to speakers of other languages* (pp. 66–71). Cambridge University Press. http://dx.doi.org/10.1017/CBO9780511667206.010

Trent, J. (2014). Innovation as identity construction in language teaching and learning: Case studies from Hong Kong. *Innovation in Language Learning and Teaching, 8*(1), 56–78. http://dx.doi.org/10.1080/17501229.2012.750664

Wassell, B., Wesely, P., & Glynn, C. (2019). Agents of change: Reimagining curriculum and instruction in world language classrooms through social justice education. *Journal of Curriculum and Pedagogy, 16*(3), 263–284. https://doi.org/10.1080/15505170.2019.1570399

Wiggins, G., & McTighe, J. (2005). *Understanding by design.* Pearson.

Varghese, M., Morgan, B., Johnston, B., & Johnson, K. (2005). Theorizing language teacher identity: Three perspectives and beyond. *Journal of Language, Identity, and Education, 4*, 21–44. http://dx.doi.org/10.1207/s15327701jlie0401_2

2 Conceptualizing Content in Unit Planning

In this chapter, I begin my presentation of practical strategies for content-driven curriculum planning in foreign language education. I describe ways of designing a thematic unit's "content nucleus," which includes a set of architectural elements that root the unit in a basis of nonlinguistic content and will later serve as a compass for integrating language. The chapter is divided into four sections: (1) choosing a thought-provoking theme that is relevant to your learners; (2) conducting research to expand your background knowledge about content and identify helpful authentic texts; (3) using the research you conducted to articulate essential questions and enduring understandings (Wiggins & McTighe, 2005); and (4) designing real-world summative assessments. Each main section includes background information on important design concepts, examples from my French teaching at the Middlebury Institute, and invitations for you to create your own curricular materials.

2.1 Themes

2.1.1 Background

Building a content-based thematic unit starts with selecting an appropriate theme. Themes are defined in the pedagogical literature as "the central ideas that organize major curricular units" (Stoller & Grabe, 2017, p. 56). According to Clementi and Terrill (2013), curricular units that are based on themes, known as "thematic units," should:

- help students develop their language proficiency;
- help students develop their intercultural competence;
- be interesting to students;

DOI: 10.4324/9781003017424-3

- be cognitively engaging; and
- be rooted in the [ACTFL] Standards (p. 26).

Themes provide "an organizing framework for a language course that transcends formal or structural requirements in a curriculum" (Brown & Lee, 2015, p. 49) and are an important tool for creating a meaningful and purposeful context for language instruction (Glisan & Donato, 2021).

There are many benefits associated with thematic unit planning. In line with CBI, it "helps students go beyond knowledge and skills in their language use and brings them to the point of actually using these skills to gain access to important ideas that are worth understanding" (Curtain & Dahlberg, 2016, p. 40). It has also been noted that thematic planning can enhance student motivation by providing interesting contexts for language learning (Clementi & Terrill, 2013; Curtain & Dahlberg, 2016; Stoller & Grabe, 2017), as well as by helping "to connect ideas and information to make them more understandable and easier to remember" (Curtain & Dahlberg, 2016, p. 42).

It is vital that thematic units be cognitively engaging to learners, that is, "substantive enough to promote systematic and reflective inquiry" (Stoller & Grabe, 2017, p. 56). In this light, Curtain and Dahlberg (2016) contrast themes with topics, claiming that the former is "a richer basis for a unit, one that has greater potential for meaning and purpose," while the latter "usually involves just a loose collection of ideas" (p. 43). Topics sit a planning rung below themes, as "subunits of content that permit the exploration of more specific aspects of the theme" (Stoller & Grabe, 2017, p. 57). When designing thematic units, Curtain and Dahlberg (2010) recommend moving from topics to themes, noting that themes are "a way of 'putting clothes on' the topic, to make it more appealing and colorful, and to give it more personality—and a much stronger affective impact" (p. 164).

To give an example, consider the common textbook theme called "food." I would argue that food represents a topic, not a theme. This topic could be expanded to a more engaging theme, such as "food (in)security in Francophone Africa." Whereas a unit on food normally includes basic food vocabulary and expressions for ordering at a restaurant, a unit on food (in)security in Francophone Africa could include explorations of interesting information and ideas related to a variety of topics, such as climate, warfare, etc. In a previous publication I referred to the process of enriching anemic textbook topics as "exploding the textbook" (Martel, 2013).

2.1.2 Example

The curricular unit I present in this book is built on the theme of "(anti)racism in Quebec." I chose this theme because:

- it allowed me to make curricular connections with the growing societal awareness of race-based issues in the United States at the time the course was offered;
- my students expressed interest in exploring it; and
- it set the groundwork for intellectual discussions on issues that are relevant to graduate students in international fields of study.

The theme addresses multiple topics, including systemic discrimination, while privilege, and strategies for combatting racism.

2.1.3 Your Turn

In consultation with your students, determine a cognitively engaging theme for a content-based thematic unit. As a starting point, you could consider exploding one of the "themes" in a commercial textbook, which may be strategic if you work in a department with many sections of the same course that relies on a textbook. Enter the theme you would like to work with into the thematic unit plan template in Appendix A.

2.2 Content Research

2.2.1 Background

With a theme in place for your thematic unit, the next step is to take stock of your content knowledge related to the theme. There is no concealing that implementing CBI requires a foundation of content knowledge. As foreign language teachers who are principally language-trained, we can start by tapping into the transdisciplinary knowledge we acquired during our undergraduate and graduate educations. For example, in a recent study, two friends and I demonstrated how a high school Spanish teacher relied on her previous liberal arts education in the domains of social studies, art, and literature to design content-based units on Spanglish and on the lives of Frida Kahlo and Diego Rivera (Troyan, Cammarata, & Martel, 2017). However, there may be times when you need to seek out new knowledge to develop a content-based thematic unit. While this may seem like a daunting prospect, it is also exciting and dovetails with calls for teachers to be continual learners (see ACTFL/CAEP, 2013; National Board for Professional Teaching Standards, 2010).

Beyond what you know already, there are many ways to expand your content knowledge related to your theme of interest. These include, but are not limited to, talking to and observing colleagues from other departments,[1] exploring content standards from other academic disciplines, and seeking out new texts to study. Of particular importance are authentic texts in the target language, which are defined as "those that are created for some real-world purpose other than language learning, and often, but not always, provided by native speakers for native speakers" (Zyzik & Polio, 2017, p. 1). As foreign language teachers, we know that authentic texts are helpful tools "for acquiring new information and accessing cultural and interdisciplinary content" (Glisan, 2012, p. 521) and for designing curriculum "that systematically incorporate[s] transcultural content and translingual reflection at every level" (MLA Ad Hoc Committee on Foreign Languages, 2007, para. 13; see also Zyzik & Polio, 2017). Furthermore, authentic texts represent an important element of the ACTFL Standards:

> [w]oven throughout the National Standards is the learner's ability to interpret authentic texts, as the vehicle for developing interpretive communication skills, understanding the products, practices, and perspectives of target cultures, making connections to other disciplines, making linguistic and cultural comparisons, and interacting in target-language communities.
>
> (Glisan, 2012, p. 52)[2]

2.2.2 *Example*

My unit on (anti)racism in Quebec is built on content knowledge that was acquired from multiple sources. First, I have done a good amount of reading about critical pedagogy and social justice for graduate school courses and personal interest (e.g., books like Sensoy and DiAngelo's [2017] *Is Everyone Really Equal?: An Introduction to Key Concepts in Social Justice* and Coates' [2017] *We Were Eight Years in Power: An American Tragedy*), so I was able to draw on that foundational knowledge. However, I did not know much about how racial issues played out in the province of Quebec, specifically. Therefore, I did multiple Google and Google Scholar searches for sources on the topic, using terms such as *racisme* (racism), *discrimination* (discrimination), *suprématie blanche* (white supremacy), *privilège blanc* (white privilege), and *Québec* (Quebec). These searches revealed several articles and videos in French that I could use in my unit, such as *Qu'est-ce que le 'privilège blanc'?* (What is 'white privilege?'; BBC News Afrique, 2020) and *Le racisme systémique, c'est quoi?* (What is systemic racism?; Le Devoir, 2020). I also studied readings such as "Interethnic relations and racism in Quebec" (Potvin, 2010) and "Awakening to white privilege and power in Canada" (Syed & Hill, 2011), which, while not in French, helped me develop my understanding of the theme. Furthermore, I consulted educational websites with advice on how to teach about racism, such as "Three essential questions about equality for your social studies class" (Rock, n.d.) and "Toolkit for teaching about racism in the context of persistent health and healthcare disparities" (Society of Teachers of Medicine, 2017).

2.2.3 Your Turn

Start by brainstorming what you know already about your chosen theme. Then, reach out to colleagues in other departments if possible to determine which aspects of their subject matter dovetail with the theme you've chosen. If possible, study their pertinent content standards (see Appendix B for a list of K–12 content standards by subject, which may come up in such discussions). With this basis in mind, generate search terms in the target language related to your theme and browse the web to identify authentic texts of interest (e.g., articles, videos, stories, radio spots). Study these texts and take note of the key information and ideas they contain. As you continue to read and view different texts, you will come across new information and ideas that will produce additional key words and direct you to additional relevant texts. You may also end up with texts that aren't in the target language but that are helpful to your learning. Continue seeking out texts until you feel like you have a sufficient grasp of your theme's content, keeping in mind that you will never be able to know everything there is to know.

This process will likely yield you a bank of authentic texts in the target language that you can use with students in your thematic unit. Analyze these texts using the procedures described on the CoBaLTT website (Regents of the University of Minnesota, n.d.) to better understand their content, cultural, and linguistic components. This analysis will help you decide which texts are ultimately a good fit for your students. Adair-Hauck, Glisan, and Troyan (2013) remind us that usable authentic texts are context-, age-, and linguistically appropriate. Importantly, linguistically appropriate texts are not ones "that have the exact grammar and vocabulary that students have learned" but instead ones that "have enough language that students can recognize so they can use these recognizable portions on which to scaffold meaning" (p. 33).

As a final step, start to think about a logical order in which you could use your identified authentic texts in your thematic unit. Graves (2000) lays out possible sequencing models:

- A is simpler or less demanding; B is more complex or more demanding.
- A is more controlled; B is more open-ended.
- A provides knowledge or skills required to do or understand B (or B builds on knowledge and skills provided by A). (p. 136)

She also mentions the sequencing principle of moving "from the individual to the home to the community to the larger world" (p. 136). Enter your findings into the content research planning guide in Appendix C.

I understand that this process may seem overly time consuming. However, I find that it takes far less time to find authentic texts that address the content I'm interested in rather than ones that include multiple examples of a specific grammar point.

2.3 Essential Questions and Enduring Understandings

2.3.1 Background

Once you have completed sufficient background research related to your theme, you are ready to articulate essential questions and enduring understandings, two core tools from the UbD framework.

Essential questions "[lie] at the heart of a subject...and [promote] inquiry and uncoverage[3] of a subject" (Wiggins & McTighe, 2005, p. 342). They:

- have no simple 'right' answer; they are meant to be argued;
- are designed to provoke and sustain student inquiry, while focusing learning and final performances;
- often address the philosophical foundations of a discipline;
- raise other important questions;
- naturally and appropriately recur; and
- stimulate vital, ongoing rethinking of big ideas, assumptions, and prior lessons (McTighe & Wiggins, 2004, p. 91).

Enduring understandings are "the specific insights, inferences, or conclusions about the big ideas that you hope your students will attain as a result of inquiry" (McTighe & Wiggins, 2013, p. 30). They:

- [involve] the Big Ideas that give meaning and importance to facts;
- can transfer to other topics, fields, and adult life;
- [are] usually not obvious; and
- [are] deliberately framed as a generalization—the 'moral of the story' (McTighe & Wiggins, 2004, p. 115).

According to Wiggins and McTighe (2005), enduring understandings are "best acquired by 'uncovering' (i.e., [they] must be developed inductively, constructed by learners) and 'doing' the subject (i.e., using the ideas in realistic settings and with real-world problems)" (p. 129).

In my experience, essential questions have become relatively popular in foreign language education. However, I have noticed that they are usually tacked on to commercial textbook themes with the primary goal of creating context for practicing language structures, supporting a language-driven approach. Instead, they should be used primarily to stimulate deep explorations of content-based information and ideas, supporting a content-driven approach. I have also noticed that enduring understandings have not been implemented as widely in foreign language education as essential questions, likely given the field's predominant focus on language development instead of content-based inquiry. When planning for CBI, enduring understandings become vital, as they represent the core of what we want our students to learn about our units' thematic content. The best example of essential questions and enduring understandings I have encountered so far in foreign language education is in Adair-Hauck et al. (2013), which contains a unit framed around questions such as "Why do people choose to leave one place and settle in another?" and corresponding takeaways such as "In many ways, the hardships experienced by Franco-Americans in New England and Maine parallel the experiences of current refugees in our community" (p. 30).

The UbD literature details methods for designing essential questions and enduring understandings, principally by unpacking them from subject area content standards (McTighe & Wiggins, 2013; Wiggins & McTighe, 2005). However, given that our curricular units are generally interdisciplinary in foreign language education, I recommend adopting a strategy of first determining enduring understandings based on your content research process and then deriving essential questions from these enduring understandings.

2.3.2 Example

My unit on (anti)racism in Quebec is built around two essential questions, which were derived during my content research process: (1) How does racism operate in Quebec? and (2) How can racism be combated in Quebec? These questions are accompanied by two enduring understandings: (1) Quebec struggles with racism, even if some say that racism is not a problem in Canada and (2) combating racism requires persistent effort and engagement in situations that will not always be comfortable.

I think it's important to note that arriving at these questions and takeaways felt at times like a messy process. My thinking changed often, as I came into contact with additional resources. Admittedly, there were moments when I felt a bit in over my head. However, I pressed on, reassuring myself that there was no "right" or "perfect" product to be grasped. I understood that the unit would only improve over time, as I did more research and implemented it over and over again. I was also comforted by the idea that the intellectual architecture I was building for the unit would be motivating and relevant to my students—much more so than the curricula in most commercial textbooks, especially at the beginning and intermediate levels of study.

2.3.3 Your Turn

Return to your content research and generate main takeaways related to your theme. These statements represent your enduring understandings. I know this can be a daunting process, but as a colleague insightfully pointed out to me, "we don't need to be content experts to come up with good enduring understandings, just curious thinkers" (C. Eagle, personal communication, February 21, 2021). Then, articulate questions that can serve as guides for arriving at the takeaways you came up with. These questions represent your essential questions. McTighe and Wiggins (2004) recommend between two and five essential questions per unit, with the caveat that less is more (and I would argue the same for enduring understandings). Enter your ideas into the thematic unit plan template in Appendix A.

2.4 Summative Performance Assessment

2.4.1 Background

The last step in designing your thematic unit's content nucleus is to create a summative assessment. Summative assessments are usually administered at the end of a unit and provide evidence of student learning related to the unit's overarching learning goals. According to Green (2014), summative assessments are those that are "concerned retrospectively with what has been learnt" (p. 241). A unit's overall assessment plan consists of both summative assessment(s) and formative assessments, the latter of which will be discussed in the next chapter. Lately, there has been an emphasis on using performance tasks as summative assessments, which are defined as "[c]omplex challenges that mirror the issues and problems faced by adults" (Wiggins & McTighe, 2005, p. 153). Performance tasks are important when planning for CBI because they illuminate student understanding; Wiggins and McTighe's (2005) "theory of understanding contends that contextualized application is the appropriate means of evoking and assessing *enduring* understandings" (p. 152, emphasis in original). In adopting a content-driven, content-based approach to curriculum design, the goal is for our students to develop deep understandings of the content we program in our thematic units in addition to the ability to use language forms communicatively.

Thankfully, we already have a summative assessment system in foreign language education that can accommodate content learning: the Integrated Performance Assessment (IPA; Adair-Hauck et al., 2006; Adair-Hauck et al., 2013). Rooted in the ACTFL Standards, the IPA consists of thematically integrated interpretive, interpersonal, and presentational tasks[4] (see Adair-Hauck et al.'s [2013] excellent manual for more information, including design specifications). Content is inherent to the IPA in that students are asked to interpret content from texts and then discuss and present about that content. There are, however, certain modifications that need to be made to more fully account for content, notably regarding rubrics (Tedick & Cammarata, n.d.; Troyan, 2016). Furthermore, interpersonal and presentational tasks can be broadened to assess content learning from across entire thematic units rather than simply the content learned or reviewed in IPA-based interpretive tasks.

When designing IPAs with content in mind, notably interpersonal and presentational tasks, it is helpful to consult Wiggins and McTighe's (2005) GRASPS framework. GRASPS can be used to elaborate the following real-world characteristics of performance tasks:

- the goal of task completion (G);
- the role(s) students fill (R);
- the intended audience for the task (A);
- the situation in which the task is contextualized (S);

- the culminating product or performance (P); and
- the standards by which task performance will be evaluated (S).

See McTighe and Wiggins' (2004) manual for further explanations and examples of GRASPS-style performance tasks. You can also consider using just one task from the IPA rather than all three, especially with shorter units. If you do this, however, think about alternating modes of communication across units within a course, e.g., by using a presentational writing task for your course's first unit, an interpersonal speaking task for your course's second unit, etc.

You have perhaps noticed that I do not mention more traditional forms of summative language assessment here, that is, ones that "primarily measure students' written accuracy in applying grammatical rules and vocabulary memorization" (Ritz, 2021, p. 86). I follow Shrum and Glisan (2016), who state that "while paper-and-pencil tests and quizzes may be adequate for assessing basic facts and skills, performance tasks are necessary for assessing deep understanding and big ideas" (p. 361). I think it is quite fine for traditional quizzes to be used as formative assessments, interspersed throughout a thematic unit, to take stock of whether your students are grasping metalinguistic knowledge about the forms and functions you are teaching. However, they are inadequate when it comes to assessing a thematic unit's ultimate content-based goals, notably its enduring understandings.

2.4.2 Example

Inspired by GRASPS, my unit on (anti)racism in Quebec includes a summative presentational writing task in the form of an op-ed piece for the Montreal newspaper *Le Devoir*. For this project, students are asked to reflect on what they've learned about racism in Quebec and use this new information to suggest directions for personal and societal action against racism in their home community(ies). This task aligns with the students' internationally focused fields of study, allows them to speak from their authentic voices, and involves a real-world audience. To prepare students for the task, I provide them with an op-ed template from the California Medical Association (n.d.) that discusses genre conventions and includes an example. I also plan time in class for the students to conduct peer reviews of a draft before submitting their final version.

In the spirit of differentiation, it could also be interesting to provide students with a menu of summative performance task options (Savage, 2015, Tomlinson, 2014). There are other ways people share their opinions on social issues of the day beyond op-eds; for example, they have conversations with their friends and create videos that they post on TikTok or YouTube. Students could therefore be given the opportunity to choose between these three genres—a presentational writing task (the op-ed), an interpersonal speaking task (a conversation), and a presentational speaking task (a YouTube video)—to demonstrate their learning from the unit.

2.4.3 Your Turn

Develop a complete IPA or one task from the IPA system to be used as your thematic unit's summative assessment, in consultation with Wiggins and McTighe's (2005) GRASPS framework. Make sure that the assessment aligns with your thematic unit's essential questions and enduring understandings. Enter your ideas into the thematic unit plan template in Appendix A.

2.5 Summary

In this chapter, I explored strategies for planning what I refer to as the content nucleus of a content-based thematic unit. I suggested the following:

- choosing a thought-provoking theme that is relevant to your learners;
- conducting research to expand your background knowledge on the theme and to identify authentic texts to use in the unit;
- using the research you conducted to design essential questions and enduring understandings, which root your unit in a process of content-based inquiry (Wiggins & McTighe, 2005); and
- designing a real-life summative performance task(s).

Looking forward, the next chapter addresses planning additional elements of a content-based thematic unit's architecture from a content and language integrated perspective.

2.6 Reflection Questions

- Which themes have you used in your curriculum? Would you consider them to be cognitively engaging?
- Which content from your previous undergraduate and graduate studies do you think would be interesting to explore with your students?

- Which content would you like to learn more about, with the goal of exploring it with your students?
- Which colleagues in other departments would you like to talk to, with the goal of learning more about what they teach?
- What role do authentic texts play in your curriculum?
- Why is inquiry—that is, "the act of questioning and the relentless search for answers to important questions that require deeper forms of thinking" (Cammarata, 2016, p. 124)—so important in education?
- What types of summative assessment do you tend to use? How communicative would you say these assessments are? Which mode(s) of communication are reflected?
- Do you evaluate students' content learning on summative assessments in addition to their language learning?

2.7 Key Resources

- *Authentic Materials Myths: Applying Second Language Research to Classroom Teaching* (Zyzik & Polio, 2017). This book contains a wealth of concrete strategies for using authentic texts in foreign language courses.
- *Enacting the Work of Language Instruction: High-Leverage Teaching Practices, Volume 2* (Glisan & Donato, 2021). This book includes chapters on creating meaningful and purposeful contexts for language instruction and backward planning.
- *Implementing Integrated Performance Assessment* (Adair-Hauck et al., 2013). This book lays out design specifications for ACTFL's IPA, for those who are interested in using it as their thematic unit's summative assessment.
- *Understanding by Design: Professional Development Workbook* (McTighe & Wiggins, 2004). This companion guide to Wiggins and McTighe (2005) contains numerous worksheets that help readers understand and implement key backward design concepts.

Notes

1 Connecting with colleagues from other departments is a great way of becoming familiar with their disciplines' core tasks, which Wiggins and McTighe (2005) define as "the most important performance demands in any field" (p. 78).
2 It should be noted that there is a range of perspectives regarding the use of authentic materials with language learners, especially beginners. As Ellis and Shintani (2014) state, "[f]rom an SLA perspective, [...] fully authentic

materials will only be of value to learners if they have reached a level of development that makes them accessible," while also adding that "[t]here is, however, the danger that simplified input will deprive learners of exposure to the wide range of linguistic features needed for full development" (p. 188). It may therefore be acceptable for you to use a mix of authentic texts with ones that have been modified or simplified in some way in your curriculum.

3 By "uncoverage," Wiggins and McTighe (2005) mean "to go into depth" in a subject (p. 352).
4 Canonically, the IPA has three tasks. I have also experimented with using a five-task version that includes interpretive reading, interpretive listening, interpersonal speaking, presentational writing, and presentational speaking tasks. See Martel and Bailey (2016) for more information.

References

ACTFL/CAEP. (2013). *ACTFL/CAEP program standards for the preparation of foreign language teachers.* https://www.actfl.org/sites/default/files/caep/ACTFLCAEPStandards2013_v2015.pdf

Adair-Hauck, B., Glisan, E., Koda, K., Swender, E., & Sandrock, P. (2006). The Integrated Performance Assessment (IPA): Connecting assessment to instruction and learning. *Foreign Language Annals, 39*(3), 359–382.

Adair-Hauck, B., Glisan, E., & Troyan, F. (2013). *Implementing Integrated Performance Assessment.* ACTFL.

BBC News Afrique. (2020, June 21). *Qu'est-ce que le 'privilège blanc'?* BBC. https://www.bbc.com/afrique/monde-53141179

Brown, H., & Lee, H. (2015). *Teaching by principles: An interactive approach to language pedagogy* (4th ed.). Pearson.

California Medical Association (n.d.). *Opinion editorial "op-ed" template.* https://championprovider.ucsf.edu/sites/champion.ucsf.edu/files/2017-09-28%20Op-ed%20template_Revised.pdf

Cammarata, L. (2016). Foreign language education and the development of inquiry-driven language programs: Key challenges and curricular planning strategies. In L. Cammarata (Ed.), *Content-based foreign language teaching: Curriculum and pedagogy for developing advanced thinking and literacy skills* (pp. 123–144). Routledge.

Clementi, D., & Terrill, L. (2013). *The keys to planning for learning: Effective curriculum, unit, and lesson design.* ACTFL.

Coates, T. (2017). *We were eight years in power: An American tragedy.* BCP Literary, Inc.

Curtain, H., & Dahlberg, C. (2010). *Languages and children: Making the match: New languages for young learners, grades K–8* (4th ed.). Pearson.

Curtain, H., & Dahlberg, C. (2016). *Learners and languages: Making the match: World language instruction in K–8 classrooms and beyond* (5th ed.). Pearson.

Ellis, R., & Shintani, N. (2014). *Exploring language pedagogy through second language acquisition research.* Routledge. http://dx.doi.org/10.1017/S0272263102002073

Glisan, E. (2012). National standards: Research into practice. *Language Teaching, 45*(4), 515–526. http://dx.doi.org/10.1017/S0261444812000249

Glisan, E., & Donato, R. (2021). *Enacting the work of language instruction: High-leverage teaching practices.* ACTFL.

Graves, K. (2000). *Designing language courses: A guide for teachers.* Heinle & Heinle.

Green, A. (2014). *Exploring language assessment and testing: Language in action.* Routledge. http://dx.doi.org/10.4324/9781315889627

Le Devoir. (2020, June 4). *Le racisme systémique, c'est quoi?* [Video]. YouTube. https://www.youtube.com/watch?v=KQBQ-OkCYyA

Martel, J. (2013). Saying our final goodbyes to the grammatical syllabus: A curricular imperative. *French Review, 86*(6), 1122–1133. http://dx.doi.org/10.1353/tfr.2013.0106

Martel, J., & Bailey, K. (2016). Exploring the trajectory of an educational innovation: Instructors' attitudes toward IPA implementation in a post-secondary intensive summer language program. *Foreign Language Annals, 49*(3), 530–543.

McTighe, J., & Wiggins, G. (2004). *Understanding by design: Professional development workbook.* ASCD.

McTighe, J., & Wiggins, G. (2013). *Essential questions: Opening doors to student understanding.* ASCD.

MLA Ad Hoc Committee on Foreign Languages. (2007). Foreign languages and higher education: New structures for a changed world. *Profession 2007,* 234–245.

National Board for Professional Teaching Standards. (2010). *World languages standards.* https://www.nbpts.org/wp-content/uploads/ECYA-WL.pdf

Potvin, M. (2010). Interethnic relations and racism in Quebec. In J. Rudy, S. Gervais, & C. Kirkey (Eds.), *Quebec questions: Quebec studies for the 21st century* (pp. 271–296). Oxford University Press.

Regents of the University of Minnesota (n.d.). *Analyzing texts.* https://carla.umn.edu/cobaltt/modules/curriculum/ta_form.html

Ritz, C. (2021). *Leading your world language program: Strategies for design and supervision, even if you don't speak the language!* Routledge.

Rock, B. (n.d.). *Three essential questions about equality for your social studies class.* The Civic Educator. https://civiceducator.org/equality-essential-questions/

Savage, J. (2015). *Lesson planning: Key concepts and skills for teachers.* Routledge. http://dx.doi.org/10.4324/9781315765181

Sensoy, Ö., & DiAngelo, R. (2017). *Is everyone really equal?: An introduction to key concepts in social justice education.* Teachers College Press.

Shrum, J., & Glisan, E. (2016). *Teacher's handbook: Contextualized language instruction* (5th ed.). Cengage.

Society of Teachers of Medicine. (2017). *Toolkit for teaching about racism in the context of persistent health and healthcare disparities.* https://resourcelibrary.stfm.org/HigherLogic/System/DownloadDocumentFile.ashx?DocumentFileKey=cf40991e-96e9-3e15-ef15-7be20cb04dc1&forceDialog=0

Stoller, F., & Grabe, W. (2017). Building coherence into the content-based curriculum: The six Ts revisited. In M. Snow & D. Brinton (Eds.), *The content-based classroom: New perspectives on integrating language and content* (pp. 53–66). University of Michigan Press.

Syed, K., & Hill, A. (2011). Awakening to white privilege and power in Canada. *Policy Futures in Education, 9*(5), 608–615. http://dx.doi.org/10.2304/pfie.2011.9.5.608

Tedick, D., & Cammarata, L. (n.d.). *Integrated Performance Assessment: Adapting the model for CBI.* https://carla.umn.edu/cobaltt/modules/assessment/ipa/index.html

Tomlinson, C. (2014). *The differentiated classroom: Responding to the needs of all learners.* ASCD.

Troyan, F. (2016). Assessing what matters within content-based foreign language teaching through Integrated Performance Assessment. In L. Cammarata (Ed.), *Content-based foreign language teaching: Curriculum and pedagogy for developing advanced thinking and literacy skills* (pp. 147–169). Routledge.

Troyan, F., Cammarata, L., & Martel, J. (2017). Integration PCK: Modeling the knowledge(s) underlying a world language teacher's implementation of CBI. *Foreign Language Annals, 50*(2), 458–476. http://dx.doi.org/10.1111/flan.12266

Wiggins, G., & McTighe, J. (2005). *Understanding by design.* Pearson.

Zyzik, E., & Polio, C. (2017). *Authentic materials myths: Applying second language research to classroom teaching.* University of Michigan Press. http://dx.doi.org/10.3998/mpub.7892433

3 Balancing Language and Content in Unit Planning

In this chapter, I continue my presentation of practical strategies for content-driven curriculum planning in foreign language education. I describe ways of designing a thematic unit's content and language integrated architecture. The chapter is divided into three sections: (1) conducting an analysis to determine possible language foci; (2) articulating knowledge and skills goals that address both content and language; and (3) rounding out the unit's assessment plan with a dual emphasis on content and language. As with the previous chapter, each main section includes background information on important design concepts, examples from my French teaching at the Middlebury Institute, and invitations for you to create your own curricular materials.

3.1 Language Analysis

3.1.1 Background

In the previous chapter, I outlined a process for conducting research to conceptualize your thematic unit's content nucleus. In this chapter, I turn to a process for analyzing the linguistic nature of your chosen content, following Tedick's (2003) claim that "the linguistic elements that make up language (i.e., grammatical structures, vocabulary, etc.) emerge naturally from the content and are understood within the context of that content" (p. 10). This work will help you construct unit-level learning goals, which will be addressed in the next main section. As far as I see it, the principal source of linguistic information is your summative assessment. Beyond this, you can consult your corpus of authentic texts, your previous curriculum, and your students. I will walk through each of these sources in turn in the following paragraphs.

DOI: 10.4324/9781003017424-4

Your unit's summative performance task is the most important source of information for determining your unit's linguistic makeup. If it is communicative in nature, the task will require the use of specific language functions. Language functions are "the communicative intentions or purposes of speakers' utterances" (Peregoy & Boyle, 2008, p. 120). For a comprehensive list of personal and academic language functions, see Tedick (n.d.). Language functions are enacted with language forms, including both grammar and vocabulary. A way of identifying which forms can fulfill which functions is to ask yourself, what is the language of [X language function]? For example, the language of comparing in English could include forms such as the comparative, the superlative, or conjunctions (see Tarone & Swierzbin, 2009). Keep in mind that there are many possible forms that can be used to accomplish a given language function. The functions and forms associated with your summative performance task represent "content-obligatory" language, which Snow, Met, and Genesee (1989) define as "the language required to develop, master, and communicate about a given content material" (pp. 205–206; see also Tedick & Lyster, 2020).

Beyond your summative performance task, you can analyze the linguistic elements in the authentic texts you collected for your thematic unit. These texts include a wealth of functions and forms that encode their intended messages. As such, it is most fruitful at this level of planning to identify functions and forms that you would consider to be content-obligatory, that are frequently recurring, and that are either new or continually challenging to your students (Lyster, 2017). Crucially, when identifying such forms, remember that students do not need to understand *all* the language in an authentic text to successfully grasp important aspects of its content.

Furthermore, you can look back to your prior curriculum. Many of the functions and forms you previously taught could likely stand to be revisited, even if they are not necessarily evoked in your current unit's summative performance task or collection of authentic texts. Such forms represent "content-compatible" language, which includes forms that "*can* be taught within the context of a given content but are *not required* for successful content mastery" (Snow et al., 1989, p. 206, emphasis in original; see also Tedick & Lyster, 2020). The idea is to contextualize these forms into your current thematic unit where possible to give students further opportunities to practice them. Incorporating content-compatible language foci recognizes that second language learning is a process, and that with many forms, both grammatical and lexical, students need multiple meaningful passes to master them (Ellis & Shintani, 2014; Schmitt, 2008; Tedick, 2003).

Finally, do not forget about your students, as they likely have in mind functions and forms that they would like to study. These language foci can be determined using common needs assessment tools, such as surveys and interviews (Graves, 2000; Nation & Macalister, 2010). They can also be determined by practicing what Han and Selinker (1999) call "empirical pedagogy" (p. 248), which asks teachers "to listen carefully to their students and to read their written work attentively with a view to identifying language difficulties that their students are experiencing" (Tedick & Lyster, 2020, p. 97; see also Snow et al., 1989). Importantly, empirical pedagogues should "give priority to language features that (a) entail recurring errors made by most students and (b) are necessary for the successful completion of tasks in specific content areas" (Tedick & Lyster, 2020, p. 97). Of course, if you are unable to obtain data from your students before your course's first meeting date, you can implement needs assessment procedures during the first unit of instruction and then use the data you collect to shape subsequent units.

These four analyses will yield quite a bit of information about the linguistic features of your unit. It will ultimately be impossible to explicitly focus on all these features within a single unit of study. The goal at this juncture, therefore, is to get an initial sense of all that is possible before making decisions about what to explicitly address in your unit.

3.1.2 Example

Table 3.1 includes findings from the analysis I conducted to determine potential language foci for my unit on (anti)racism in Quebec. The forms provided by the students were solicited using a needs assessment survey that was administered during the first week of the course.

3.1.3 Your Turn

Consult as many of the four sources of information identified above as possible to generate potential language foci for your thematic unit. Enter your findings into the language analysis planning guide in Appendix D.

Table 3.1 Possible language foci for my unit on (anti)racism in Quebec

Information Source	Potential Language Foci

Summative Performance Task (op-ed in *Le Devoir*)	• Function: Making suggestions
	• Forms:
	  • Conditional forms of *devoir* (should)
	  • The subjunctive, e.g., *il faut que...* (it is necessary that...)
	  • Vocabulary items such as *racisme* (racism), *systémique* (systemic), *privilège* (privilege)

Authentic Texts[1]	• Functions:
	  • Defining terms
	  • Explaining real-world application of concepts
	  • Highlighting important information
	• Forms:
	  • *X, c'est des...* (X is/are...)
	  • *Si on veut parler de X, on dit...* (talking about X means...)
	  • *Il est important de...* (it's important to...)
	  • Vocabulary items such as *discriminatoire* (discriminatory), *taux de chômage* (unemployment rate), *racisé* (racialized)

Prior Curriculum	• Function: Comparing/contrasting
	• Forms:
	  • Conjunctions, e.g., *et* (and), *mais* (but)
	  • Adjective structures, e.g., *plus XXX que* (more XXX than)
	  • Noun structures, e.g., *moins de XXX que* (less XXX than)

Students	• Forms:
	  • Pronouns
	  • Past tenses
	  • The future
	  • The conditional
	  • Question forms

3.2 Learning Goals

3.2.1 Background

Thanks to the work you've done so far, you are ready to develop content and language integrated learning goals for your thematic unit.

Learning goals can be parsed into two domains: skills and knowledge. According to Wiggins and McTighe (2005), these two constructs represent "the building blocks for the desired understandings" (p. 57). As such, it is helpful to ask yourself, which skills and knowledge do my students need to successfully grasp my thematic unit's enduring understandings? The answer to this question will help you articulate skills and knowledge goals. Let's discuss both types of goals in turn, starting with skills. I find it helpful to start with skills because in most cases, knowledge serves as a resource for enacting skills. Language is a great example; it is now well accepted in foreign language education that metalinguistic knowledge about language is a resource that students can draw on to enact communicative skills such as describing, comparing, etc. (Celce-Murcia, 1991; Hall, 2001; Liamkina & Ryshina-Pankova, 2012; Paesani, Allen, & Dupuy, 2016).

Skills represent what students are able to do. There are a variety of sources you can consult to determine relevant skills goals. From a general perspective, there's Bloom's Taxonomy, which outlines thinking skills that range from the more basic (e.g., define) to the more complex (e.g., critique). Specific to foreign language education, the ACTFL Standards represent overarching skills that can be broken down into more discrete ones. For example, the second communication standard, which reads broadly as the ability to "understand, interpret, and analyze what is heard, read, or viewed on a variety of topics" (National Standards Collaborative Board, 2015, para. 3), can be localized as a skill goal into a thematic unit as something like "students will be able to interpret authentic texts related to food (in)security in Francophone Africa." Arguably, all of ACTFL's Standards should be considered when designing thematic units, which is well demonstrated in Clementi and Terrill's (2013) sample unit on balanced lifestyles for a novice-level French class.

Furthermore, foreign language educators are taking a greater interest in the "21st Century Skills," defined as "the knowledge, life skills, career skills, habits, and traits that are critically important to student success in today's world, particularly as students move on to college, the workforce, and adult life" (Buckle, n.d.). ACTFL's *21st Century Skills Map* includes 12 categories, each of which consists of a set of specific skills:

- communication
- collaboration
- critical thinking and problem solving
- creativity and innovation
- information literacy

- media literacy
- technology literacy
- flexibility and adaptability
- initiative and self-direction
- social and cross-cultural skills
- productivity and accountability
- leadership and responsibility (P21, 2011)

To give an example, "acting responsibly with the interests of the larger community in mind" (p. 20) is a skill that falls within the category of leadership and responsibility.

Let's now return to the other element of Wiggins and McTighe's (2005) building blocks: knowledge. Knowledge includes "the facts," "a body of coherent facts," or "verifiable claims"—that is, what emerges when we "respond on cue with what [we] know" (Wiggins & McTighe, 2005, p. 38). Relevant knowledge goals are best unpacked from the content research and language analysis you conducted for your thematic unit. According to McTighe and Wiggins (2004), knowledge goals could include:

- vocabulary
- terminology
- definitions
- key factual information
- formulas
- critical details
- important events and people
- sequence and timelines (p. 119)

From a foreign language education perspective, metalinguistic knowledge—i.e., knowledge about target language structures—needs to be added to this list (Heineke & McTighe, 2018). As stated above, metalinguistic knowledge is a key resource that students draw on to enact language functions and ultimately process content.

Importantly, skills and knowledge goals are where content and language come together in integration (Heineke & McTighe, 2018). Take the Bloom's Taxonomy verb of comparing as an example. When students compare two things, they rely on content knowledge associated with those things (e.g., comparing food aid policies across Francophone countries in different regions). Furthermore, they are enacting a language function, which is supported by knowledge about language. Students cannot express the content without recourse to language, and language needs the context of content to be meaningful.

3.2.2 Example

As a result of participating in my unit on (anti)racism in Quebec, students will be able to:

- interpret and discuss authentic texts related to racism in Quebec;
- define key concepts associated with racism;
- explain cultural perspectives associated with racism in Quebec;
- synthesize information about the state of affairs of racism in Quebec; and
- express personal and societal goals for combating racism.

Furthermore, they will know:

- key concepts like (systemic) racism, whiteness, intersectionality, xenophobia, etc.;
- ways in which systemic racism operates in Quebec;
- important legal tenets regarding policing and race in Quebec;
- key statistics regarding racial profiling in Quebec;
- various methods for combating systemic racism;
- key vocabulary related to (anti)racism in Quebec;
- conjugation rules for the conditional; and
- usage rules for the conditional.

These learning goals were generated in consultation with my content research, my language analysis, and the resources mentioned in this section, such as the ACTFL Standards. They are designed specifically to help students succeed on the unit's summative assessment, thus revealing their grasp of the unit's enduring understandings. Given that the unit lasts only three weeks (with three lessons per week), I focus on just one grammar form, the conditional, which I identified as a potential goal in my analysis of the unit's summative performance task as well as by surveying my students. Note linkages between the skills and knowledge goals, that is, how the knowledge encapsulated in the knowledge goals helps students enact the skills encapsulated in the skills goals.

3.2.3 Your Turn

Consult your content research, your language analysis, and the resources mentioned in this section to articulate skills and knowledge goals to include in your thematic unit. Begin the former with the starter "Students will be able to…" and the latter with the starter "Students will know..." (McTighe & Wiggins, 2004, p. 119). When writing skills goals, I find it helpful to use active verbs from Bloom's Taxonomy (see, e.g., Shabatura, 2014).

Given all the possible language foci you identified in your analysis and the time you have allotted to your unit, it is likely you will have to do a fair amount of paring down when conceptualizing your unit's learning goals. For example, you may not always have the time to incorporate content-compatible language foci (Snow et al., 1989) from previous units into your current unit. At a minimum, make sure to include the skills and knowledge associated with your summative performance task because it is vital that your curriculum prepares your students for success on this assessment (see Sultana, 2018 for more on this principle, known as curriculum alignment). Enter your skills and knowledge goals into the thematic unit plan template in Appendix A.

3.3 Additional Assessment Planning

3.3.1 Background

In the previous chapter, you designed a summative performance assessment for your thematic unit, consisting of all or part of an Integrated Performance Assessment (IPA; Adair-Hauck, Glisan, & Troyan, 2013). It is now time to determine the content and language integrated criteria that you will use to evaluate your students' performance on that assessment, as well as the content and language integrated formative assessment procedures you will use throughout the unit, rounding out your overall assessment plan. I will address these two main areas in the paragraphs that follow.

As noted in the previous chapter, the final S of GRASPS involves outlining standards for success associated with your summative performance task (Wiggins & McTighe, 2005). Commonly referred to as criteria, these standards are the benchmarks that will guide you in evaluating student performance and giving feedback. Helpfully, the IPA framework already contains rubrics that include multiple criteria, such as language control, comprehensibility, etc. I recommend developing your own set of criteria for your summative performance task(s), however, primarily because the IPA rubrics do not explicitly address content (Tedick & Cammarata, n.d.; Troyan, 2016).

Once defined, evaluative criteria are often plugged into a grading rubric. If you need a refresher on designing rubrics, Shrum and Glisan (2016) provide a helpful set of steps, which include determining your criteria, deciding the number of levels of performance, elaborating performance descriptions by level, presenting the rubric to students, and piloting/revising the rubric. Additional information about rubrics can be found on the Virtual Assessment Center website designed by CARLA at the University of Minnesota (Regents of the University of Minnesota, n.d.). Lately, I have been using an approach to grading called "specifications grading" (Nilson, 2015). In specifications grading, students either successfully meet the criteria included in rubrics or they don't; there are no partial gradations (e.g., "weekly meets expectations"). When using this type of evaluation mechanism, I give the students multiple opportunities to revise and resubmit their work. I highly recommend reading Nilson's (2015) book; it has encouraged me to set more rigorous standards for my students and to place a greater emphasis on feedback and learning through the revise and resubmit process.

With evaluative criteria in place for your unit's summative performance assessment, it is time to turn to formative assessment. Formative assessment is defined as "educational assessment that is intended to guide the teaching and learning process" (Green, 2014, p. 233). Formative assessments help teachers monitor student learning throughout lessons and make decisions about future teaching, and as such are often referred to as "assessment *for* learning" (Clementi & Terrill, 2013, p. 37, emphasis in original; see also Wiggins & McTighe, 2005). According to Wiggins and McTighe (2005), "ongoing formative assessments are vital to reveal students' understanding and misunderstanding" (p. 169).

Frey and Fisher (2011) state that the purpose of formative assessment is "[t]o reduce discrepancies between current understanding/performance and a desired goal" (p. 3). They see formative assessment as a system that indicates to students where they are going (known as "feed-up"), how they are doing (known as "feedback"), and where they are going next (known as "feed-forward") (see Hattie, 2009). Systematicity is also a key element of Frey and Fisher's (2011) framework. As Green (2014) notes, "[t]he successful use of formative assessment depends on embedding regular procedures in the classroom" (p. 29).

Foreign language teachers are already comfortable using a variety of formative assessment tools (see Clementi & Terrill, 2013, for example, T.A.L.K. scores and exit slips). While many of these tools focus primarily on language, it is important to understand that content learning needs to be considered as well (Heineke & McTighe, 2018). For example, if you use the mechanism of a weekly quiz, you should include questions about content taught in the unit and give feedback on content learning in addition to the grammar structures and vocabulary addressed during the week.

Thankfully, many of the formative assessment techniques commonly used in foreign language education can be used to monitor both content and language learning. For example, you could ask students to share their thoughts in an exit slip about a content concept you taught during a lesson and give feedback not only on their grasp of the concept, but also on the language they used to express their thinking.[2] Indeed, any strategy used to assess content learning will also shed light upon language learning, as language is a necessary tool for students to reveal their thinking. There will be times, however, when you may want to use a strategy that focuses solely on language, such as T.A.L.K. scores (see Clementi & Terrill, 2013). If so, it is important to make sure that the majority of the strategies in your formative assessment plan address both content and language.

3.3.2 Example

Table 3.2 includes the evaluative criteria that correspond with the op-ed summative performance task in my unit on (anti)racism in Quebec, elaborated into a specifications grading-style rubric (Nilson, 2015). If students fully meet criteria, they are given full marks, i.e., one point per criterion. If they don't meet criteria, they are given no marks, i.e., no points. They then have the option to revise and resubmit their work to meet any criteria that they missed.

The following are the formative assessment procedures I use during the unit:

- observations of student content and language performance during class across interpersonal, interpretive, and presentational modes of communication[3];
- brief vocabulary quizzes at the end of synchronous sessions; and
- homework activities completed on Canvas.

I'll end this subsection with some additional clarifications about my formative assessment procedures. As is the case with many teachers, a key strategy is observation during class (McMillan, 2018). Observations allow me to determine whether students are understanding the unit's key concepts and how much scaffolding they might need to clear up any misunderstandings. While observing, I note any gaps in understanding so that they can be addressed in subsequent lessons. Furthermore, I use homework assignments to monitor student learning. For example, in preparation for the summative op-ed task, I ask

Table 3.2 Rubric for my unit's summative op-ed performance task

Criteria	Full Marks	No Marks
You demonstrate a sophisticated understanding of (anti)racism in Quebec	1 point	0 points
You provide a minimum of two pertinent pieces of information about (anti)racism in Quebec learned from the texts we studied in class	1 point	0 points
You provide a minimum of one new piece of information about (anti)racism in Quebec learned from your own personal research	1 point	0 points
You adhere to accepted genre conventions for op-eds	1 point	0 points
You correctly use a minimum of two new vocabulary words from the class Quizlet[4]	1 point	0 points
You correctly use a minimum of two conditional forms when making suggestions for personal and societal action	1 point	0 points
Total	_____/6 points	

students to write three sentences expressing how they aspire to act personally in response to documented accounts of racism in Quebec. These sentences give me the opportunity to provide feedback not only about students' language use, but also about the accuracy of their information and ideas, grounded in the content imparted in the unit's authentic texts.

3.3.3 *Your Turn*

Articulate evaluative criteria for your summative performance task(s) that encapsulate both content and language and incorporate them into a grading rubric. Then, decide which formative assessment techniques you would like to use to keep tabs on student content and language learning throughout the unit. Enter your ideas into the thematic unit plan template in Appendix A.

3.4 Summary

In this chapter, I explored strategies for conceptualizing the content and language integrated facets of a thematic unit. I suggested the following:

• conducting an analysis to determine possible language foci that emerge from content and students rather than from a predetermined syllabus (Tedick, 2003);

- articulating knowledge and skills goals to guide the unit that address content and language in an integrated fashion; and
- rounding out the unit's assessment plan with elements that address both content and language, notably criteria for the summative performance task(s) and formative assessment procedures.

Looking forward, the next chapter addresses the third phase of Wiggins and McTighe's (2005) backward planning framework, lesson planning, from a content and language integrated perspective.

3.5 Reflection Questions

- How do you decide which language forms to focus on in your curriculum?
- How do you keep track of patterns of error in your students' language interpretation and production?
- Which language forms do you notice your students struggling with the most?
- How do you use Bloom's Taxonomy in your curriculum?
- How do you use the ACTFL Standards in your curriculum?
- How does your curriculum prepare students to be 21st century learners?
- How do you feel about specifications grading? How does it compare to how you normally construct rubrics?
- Which formative assessment strategies do you tend to use? How effective are they at helping you keep tabs on student learning?

3.6 Key Resources

- *The Formative Assessment Action Plan: Practical Steps to More Successful Teaching and Learning* (Frey & Fisher, 2011). This book characterizes formative assessment as a system of interconnected facets and details many useful information-gathering strategies.
- *Understanding by Design: Professional Development Workbook* (McTighe & Wiggins, 2004). This companion guide to Wiggins and McTighe (2005) contains numerous worksheets that help readers understand and implement key backward design concepts.
- *Scaffolding Language Development in Immersion and Dual Language Classrooms* (Tedick & Lyster, 2020). Destined for dual language and immersion teachers, this robust volume digs deeply into the interface between language and content. The fourth part of the book focuses on curriculum planning and assessment.

Notes

1 This example includes functions and forms from one of the texts used in the unit: *Qu'est-ce que le racisme et la discrimination systémiques?* (What are racism and systemic discrimination?; Office de consultation publique de Montréal, 2019). Remember, however, that the idea is to look across all the texts in the unit to identify patterns of functions and forms that you would consider to be content-obligatory, frequently recurring, and either new or continually challenging to your students.

2 Especially at the novice level, there may be times where you want to use your students' first language(s) to formatively assess their content knowledge.

3 It is important that all three modes of communication be formatively assessed across a unit. Research has shown that teachers tend to favor some modes over others (Kissau & Adams, 2016).

4 Quizlet is a digital tool that is commonly used to manage vocabulary learning. See https://quizlet.com/ for more information.

References

Adair-Hauck, B., Glisan, E., & Troyan, F. (2013). *Implementing Integrated Performance Assessment*. ACTFL.

Buckle, J. (n.d.). *A comprehensive guide to 21st century skills*. Panorama Education. https://www.panoramaed.com/blog/comprehensive-guide-21st-century-skills

Celce-Murcia, M. (1991). Grammar pedagogy in second and foreign language teaching. *TESOL Quarterly*, *25*, 459–480.

Clementi, D., & Terrill, L. (2013). *The keys to planning for learning: Effective curriculum, unit, and lesson design*. ACTFL.

Ellis, R., & Shintani, N. (2014). *Exploring language pedagogy through second language acquisition research*. Routledge. http://dx.doi.org/10.4324/9780203796580

Frey, N., & Fisher, D. (2011). *The formative assessment action plan: Practical steps to more successful teaching and learning*. ASCD.

Graves, K. (2000). *Designing language courses: A guide for teachers*. Heinle & Heinle.

Green, A. (2014). *Exploring language assessment and testing: Language in action*. Routledge.

Hall, J. K. (2001). *Methods for teaching foreign languages: Creating a community of learners in the classroom*. Pearson.

Han, Z. H., & Selinker, L. (1999). Error resistance: Towards an empirical pedagogy. *Language Teaching Research*, *3*(3), 248–275. http://dx.doi.org/10.1177/136216889900300304

Hattie, J. (2009). *Visible learning: A synthesis of over 800 meta-analyses relating to achievement*. Routledge.

Heineke, A., & McTighe, J. (2018). *Using Understanding by Design in the culturally and linguistically diverse classroom*. ASCD.

Kissau, S., & Adams, M. (2016). Instructional decision making and IPAs: Assessing the modes of communication. *Foreign Language Annals, 49*(1), 105–123. http://dx.doi.org/10.1111/flan.12184

Liamkina, O., & Ryshina-Pankova, M. (2012). Grammar dilemma: Teaching grammar as a resource for making meaning. *Modern Language Journal, 92*(2), 270–289. http://dx.doi.org/10.1111/j.1540-4781.2012.01333_1.x

Lyster, R. (2017). Language-focused instruction in content-based classrooms. In M. Snow & D. Brinton (Eds.), *The content-based classroom: New perspectives on integrating language and content* (pp. 109–123). University of Michigan Press.

McMillan, J. (2018). *Classroom assessment: Principles and practice that enhance student learning and motivation* (7th ed.). Pearson.

McTighe, J., & Wiggins, G. (2004). *Understanding by design: Professional development workbook*. ASCD.

Nation, I., & Macalister, J. (2010). *Language curriculum design*. Routledge.

National Standards Collaborative Board. (2015). *World-readiness standards for learning languages* (4th ed.). Author.

Nilson, L. (2015). *Specifications grading: Restoring rigor, motivating students, and saving faculty time*. Stylus Publishing.

Office de consultation publique de Montréal. (2019, June 12). *Qu'est-ce que le racisme et la discrimination systémiques?* [Video]. YouTube. https://www.youtube.com/watch?v=S66lC9XbDMU

P21 (2011). *21st century skills map*. https://www.actfl.org/sites/default/files/resources/21st%20Century%20Skills%20Map-World%20Languages.pdf

Paesani, K., Allen, H, & Dupuy, B. (2016). *A multiliteracies framework for collegiate foreign language teaching*. Pearson.

Peregoy, S., & Boyle, O. (2008). *Reading, writing, and learning in ESL: A resource book for teaching K–12 English learners* (2nd ed.). Pearson. http://dx.doi.org/10.5054/tj.2011.244400

Regents of the University of Minnesota (n.d.). *Continuous improvement: Rubrics*. https://carla.umn.edu/assessment/vac/improvement/p_4.html

Schmitt, N. (2008). Instructed second language vocabulary learning. *Language Teaching Research, 12*(3), 329–363.

Shabatura, J. (2014). *Bloom's taxonomy verb chart*. https://tips.uark.edu/blooms-taxonomy-verb-chart/

Shrum, J., & Glisan, E. (2016). *Teacher's handbook: Contextualized language instruction* (5th ed.). Cengage.

Snow, M., Met, M., & Genesee, F. (1989). A conceptual framework for the integration of language and content instruction. *TESOL Quarterly, 23*(2), 201–217.

Sultana, N. (2018). Investigating the relationship between washback and curriculum alignment: A literature review. *Canadian Journal for New Scholars in Education, 9*(2), 151–158.

Tarone, E., & Swierzbin, B. (2009). *Exploring learner language*. Oxford University Press.

Tedick, D. (n.d.). *Communicative and academic functions.* https://carla.umn.edu/cobaltt/modules/curriculum/textanalysis/Communicative_Academic_Functions.pdf

Tedick, D. (2003). CAPRII: Key concepts to support standards-based and content-based second language instruction. *CoBaLTT Web Resource Center.* https://carla.umn.edu/cobaltt/modules/strategies/CAPRII/READING1/CAPRII.HTM

Tedick, D., & Cammarata, L. (n.d.). *Integrated Performance Assessment: Adapting the model for CBI.* https://carla.umn.edu/cobaltt/modules/assessment/ipa/index.html

Tedick, D., & Lyster, R. (2020). *Scaffolding language development in immersion and dual language classrooms.* Routledge. http://dx.doi.org/10.4324/9780429428319

Troyan, F. (2016). Assessing what matters within content-based foreign language teaching through Integrated Performance Assessment. In L. Cammarata (Ed.), *Content-based foreign language teaching: Curriculum and pedagogy for developing advanced thinking and literacy skills* (pp. 147–169). Routledge.

Wiggins, G., & McTighe, J. (2005). *Understanding by design.* Pearson.

4   Balancing Language and Content in Lesson Planning

In this chapter, I complete my presentation of practical strategies for content-driven curriculum planning in foreign language education. I describe ways of designing content and language integrated lesson plans, which fit into a thematic unit's content nucleus and content and language integrated architecture. The chapter is divided into three sections: (1) articulating learning objectives, (2) designing activities in logical sequences, and (3) performing quality control on the unit as a whole. As with Chapters 2 and 3, each main section includes background information on important design concepts, examples from my French teaching at the Middlebury Institute, and invitations for you to create your own curricular materials.

4.1 Objectives

4.1.1 Background

An essential first step in designing a lesson plan is to articulate learning objectives. Objectives represent lesson-level learning targets, and collectively, they feed into a thematic unit's overarching learning goals. Importantly, thinking about objectives does not stop once they are initially articulated. According to Shrum and Glisan (2016),

> …it is important to keep in mind that planning a lesson does not always occur in a linear process; that is, teachers sometimes begin with a learning objective, begin to plan activities, and then realize that they need to alter the objective. Sometimes a classroom activity or authentic text provides an idea for a lesson objective and a way to address a particular student standard. Therefore, planning can be more appropriately viewed as an iterative process.

(p. 99)

DOI: 10.4324/9781003017424-5

Along these lines, Wiggins and McTighe (2005) point out that there are multiple "doorways" to effective curriculum design, meaning that planning does not always need to occur in the lockstep three-stage backward process. For example, an engaging activity that you've previously used in your teaching may represent the starting point for your planning.

It is generally accepted that objectives should be "written in terms of what the learner can do" (Clementi & Terrill, 2013, p. 48), hence the common starter SWBAT, which stands for "students will be able to" (Curtain & Dahlberg, 2016; Shrum & Glisan, 2016). It is also generally accepted that objectives be "S.M.A.R.T.," which stands for specific, measurable, achievable, relevant, and time-oriented (Wayne State University, n.d.). Based on these criteria, there are certain words to avoid when writing objectives; Shrum and Glisan (2016) point out that "[v]erbs such as 'learn' or 'understand' are too vague" (p. 96).

Objectives in content-based lessons should address both content and language and be integrated where possible. However, sometimes lessons will focus more on language or more on content, especially if the time allotted per lesson is limited. For example, in a 45-minute lesson, you may implement an inductive activity focused on a language structure, meaning that the lesson is governed primarily by a language-related objective. Then, in a subsequent 45-minute lesson, you may have students use that form to talk about a content-based concept, meaning that the lesson is governed by an integrated content and language objective.

To be S.M.A.R.T., objectives should be written using verbs from Bloom's Taxonomy. Many of these verbs represent language functions, which were defined in the previous chapter as "the communicative intentions or purposes of speakers' utterances" (Peregoy & Boyle, 2008, p. 120). Following the "formula" described in Tedick and Lyster (2020), integrated content and language objectives can be designed by associating language structures and vocabulary with functions, e.g., "SWBAT compare/contrast food policies in various Francophone countries using conjunctions such as *mais* (but) and *et* (and)." Keep in mind that language objectives do not always need to target morphosyntax and vocabulary; they can also include features such as pragmatics and learning strategies (see Abrams, 2016 and Flowerdew & Miller, 2005, respectively).

4.1.2 Example

Table 4.1 contains the sequence of objectives for the nine lessons in my unit on (anti)racism in Quebec. Each lesson consists of one hour

Table 4.1 Sequence of lesson objectives for my unit on (anti)racism in Quebec

Lessons	Objective(s)
First Lesson	• SWBAT articulate initial perceptions of cultural values associated with racism in Quebec
Second Lesson	• SWBAT define racism and systemic discrimination
Third Lesson	• SWBAT define white privilege
	• SWBAT explain how to conjugate and use the conditional
Fourth Lesson	• SWBAT characterize the state of racism in Quebec and Canada
	• SWBAT articulate personal goals for combating racism using the conditional
Fifth Lesson	• SWBAT summarize strategies for combating racism
	• SWBAT explain how to use *devoir* (to have to) in the conditional
Sixth Lesson	• SWBAT summarize strategies for combating racism
	• SWBAT articulate societal goals for combating racism using the conditional
Seventh Lesson	• SWBAT further characterize the state of racism in Quebec and Canada
	• SWBAT articulate similarities and differences between racism in Quebec and in their home countries/regions
Eighth Lesson	• SWBAT request information regarding the state of racism in Quebec
Ninth Lesson	• SWBAT articulate personal and societal goals for combating racism using the conditional

of synchronous class time plus asynchronous homework to be completed before the next synchronous session. Notice how the objectives address both content and language and build on each other across the unit, preparing students for success on the summative performance task.

4.1.3 Your Turn

Decide how many lessons you will devote to your thematic unit. Then, articulate learning objectives for the lessons that guide learners through the unit in a scaffolded way to successful completion of the summative performance task. Look to the bank of authentic texts you collected for the unit for inspiration; the content-based concepts and language forms they contain could be realized into content and language objectives. Furthermore, consider how your succession of objectives reflects the "story" you are aspiring to tell in your unit or the problem you are examining (Egan, 1986; see also Curtain & Dahlberg, 2016; Wiggins & McTighe, 2005). For example, you might program objectives geared toward defining and explaining toward the beginning of the unit, which set the scene for your theme, while using objectives geared toward analyzing and creating later on, with the goal of resolving the unit's core problem/challenge. Enter your work into the lesson objectives planning guide in Appendix E.

4.2 Activities in Sequence

4.2.1 Background

Now that you know which specific learning targets will frame your unit's individual lessons, it's time to start populating the lessons with activities. A key consideration here is sequencing. The pedagogical consensus is that a lesson's activities should be organized into phases, each of which has a different function. Based on the user-friendly and flexible models from Brown and Lee (2015) and Savage (2015), I propose the following three lesson phases: an opening phase, a main phase, and a closing phase. Let's address the functions of these phases in turn.

According to Savage (2015), opening phases have three principal characteristics: to engage students, set the pace, and impart challenge. The beginnings of lessons should include a warm-up "to help students make the transition from their previous activity to the language class" and "introduce the lesson for the day, and inform the students so they know the objectives of the lesson" (Curtain & Dahlberg, 2016, p. 57). Both the beginnings and ends of lessons are good places to implement routines, such as sharing lesson objectives or explaining homework, which "make heavy use of language repetition and patterned teacher-student interaction" (Curtain & Dahlberg, 2016, p. 61).

Main phases constitute the meat of a lesson, as they contain activities that directly target the lesson's learning objective(s). The goal of main activities is to "help students to *explore* the Big Ideas and Essential Questions" and "*equip* [them] for their final performances" through a balance of experiential and inductive learning, direct instruction, and homework (Wiggins & McTighe, 2005, p. 219; emphases in original). Main activities should also capture students' attention and ask them to rethink and evaluate their own and their peers' work (Wiggins & McTighe, 2005). Activities planned in this phase should be purposeful, dynamic, and differentiated (Savage, 2015), as well as varied, especially when working with younger learners (Curtain &

Dahlberg, 2016). Naturally, there will be quite a bit of diversity in how main phases are constructed across a unit's lessons.

Finally, closing phases should accomplish the following, according to Savage (2015):

- drawing together the whole group and providing a helpful sense of community as the lesson closes;
- helping the group of students summarise and take stock of the learning that has been achieved both individually and corporately;
- providing opportunities for the extension of learning through homework or other learning opportunities;
- signposting [i.e., explicitly explaining] future learning in the next lesson or teaching episode; and
- highlighting not only what pupils have learnt but also how they have learnt it (p. 46).[1]

Similarly, Curtain and Dahlberg (2016) call for a closing activity that "could be the culminating activity of the lesson, or an opportunity for students to demonstrate their new learning" (p. 57). As such, the ends of lessons provide a good opportunity for collecting formative assessment data.

The pedagogical literature in foreign language education includes several sequencing models that can be incorporated into the three-part structure just explained, primarily as main activities (see Table 4.2). Crucially, the sequences suggested in these models do not need to fit into one lesson; rather, they can be distributed across multiple lessons, especially shorter ones. For example, if using Lyster's (2017) model, you could program noticing and awareness activities as the main activities for an initial lesson, guided practice activities as the main activities for a subsequent lesson, and autonomous practice activities as the main activities for the lesson after that. Following the three-part lesson structure, these main activities would be sandwiched by relevant opening and closing activities.

4.2.2 Example

Table 4.3 details the procedures for the second lesson of my unit on (anti)racism in Quebec, which is intended for a 60-minute synchronous class session. Consider how the opening and closing activities employ routines, such as asking students what news they have and previewing the homework (Curtain & Dahlberg, 2016), while the main activities feed directly into the lesson's objective. Also, note how I employ the

Table 4.2 Sequencing models in foreign language education

Source	Model Focus	Summary
Glisan and Donato (2017)[2]	Interpreting authentic texts	• Pre-listening/reading/viewing activities (e.g., activating schema, previewing important vocabulary) • Literal interpretation activities (e.g., supporting details) • Figurative interpretation activities (e.g., inference questions) • Creative activities
Glisan and Donato (2017)	Exploring cultural perspectives in images	• Fact questions activities • Additional information activities • Hypothesis activities • Perspectives exploration/ reflection activities
Lyster (2017)	Integrating language and content	• Noticing activities • Awareness activities • Guided practice activities • Autonomous practice activities
Paesani, Allen, and Dupuy (2016)	Relating skills instruction to written and aural texts	Depends on targeted skill (this example pertains to speaking): • Pre-speaking activities • Textual interpretation activities • Knowledge application activities • Summary and reflection activities

initial noticing component of Lyster's (2017) content and language integration model.

4.2.3 *Your Turn*

Enter the lesson objectives you designed into the lesson plan template in Appendix F, creating a new file for each lesson. Then, populate each lesson with activities that align with the objectives and fit into the three-phase structure. State the procedures using imperative verb forms. According to Hall (2001),

Table 4.3 The second lesson in my unit on (anti)racism in Quebec

---

Objective
SWBAT define racism and systemic discrimination
Procedures

Opening Activities	• Welcome students to class. Ask them how they are doing and if there is any news they'd like to share with the group.
	• Share the lesson's objectives and agenda of activities for the hour.
Main Activities	• Put students in groups to discuss their answers to the questions assigned for homework. Regroup in plenary to go over the answers, providing feedback where necessary.
	• Give students a few minutes to reflect on instances in their own lives during which they've witnessed or experienced racism. Put them in groups to discuss their thoughts. If they're not comfortable doing so, they can listen to and ask questions of their group members. Remind them to express their experiences using the *passé composé* (compound past), e.g., *j'ai témoigné* (I witnessed), *j'ai vécu* (I lived/experienced). Regroup in plenary and ask for volunteers to share what they learned from their partners.
	• Display a couple sentences that encapsulate your own aspirations for combatting racism, like the ones below. Check students' understanding of the sentences and explain why you chose them.
	• *Je **voudrais** être un(e) allié(e) pour les gens racisés.* (I would like to be an ally for racialized people.)
	• *J'**aimerais** rechercher des statistiques sur le racisme dans mon domaine professionnel.* (I would like to research statistics about racism in my professional domain.)
	• Tell the students that you'll be exploring how to use structures like the ones bolded in these sentences during the unit. Ask them to provide examples of when they've heard or seen this form before.
Closing Activities	• Revisit the unit's essential questions and ask students to share their preliminary answers.
	• Tell the students that for homework they'll watch a video about white privilege. Ask them to share what they know already about the topic.
	• Explain the homework.

...[s]ince the plan serves as a script for teacher action, the steps themselves are most easily written as directives such as 'Have students get into small groups' or 'Ask them to follow along as I read the directions aloud to them.'

(p. 110)

Remember, the process of designing activities is iterative, meaning you may end up wanting to modify some of the objectives you initially wrote as you work through the unit (Shrum & Glisan, 2016). This is quite okay; what's most important is that, in the end, your objectives and activities systematically align with each other.

In addition to your lesson's procedures, include the homework you plan to assign in between classes, if applicable. The lesson plan template also has space for you to document the information you learn from your formative assessment procedures, as well as any critical reflections geared toward improving the lesson for future use.

4.3 Quality Control

4.3.1 Background

Once you have drafted your unit's lessons, it is helpful to look back at them as a whole to make sure they reflect principles of effective (language) curriculum design. Thankfully, there are two frameworks that can facilitate this process. The first, WHERETO, is meant for teachers of all subject areas. WHERETO "seek[s] to highlight the considerations for design that follow from the logic of backward design and the nature of understanding" (Wiggins & McTighe, 2005, p. 192). WHERETO is based on the following questions:

- **Where** are we going? **Why**? **What** is expected? (W)
- How will we **hook** and **hold** student interest? (H)
- How will we **equip** students for expected performances? (E)
- How will we help students **rethink** and **revise**? (R)
- How will students self-**evaluate** and reflect on their learning? (E)
- How will we **tailor** learning to varied needs, interests, and styles? (T)
- How will we **organize** and sequence the learning? (O; McTighe & Wiggins, 2004, p. 214, emphasis in original)

WHERETO serves as "a checklist for building and evaluating the final learning plan, not a suggested sequence" (McTighe & Wiggins, 2004,

p. 214). The idea is therefore not to design W activities, then move to H activities, then to E activities, etc. Rather, it is to consider how each element of WHERETO is present across a full unit. For example, you could tell your students an engaging content-related story at the beginning of a unit to capture their attention, reflecting the H category. Then, at various other points throughout the unit, you could ask them to share their own connections and experiences with the subject matter, which also reflects the H category (see McTighe & Wiggins, 2004).

The second framework, CAPRII, can also be used to evaluate a unit to make sure it reflects principles of effective learning, with an emphasis on language. CAPRII consists of a set of six guiding concepts that are "interrelated and inseparable in effective language teaching" (Tedick, 2003, p. 3). The six concepts are contextualization of grammar, authenticity (of text and task), process, reflection, interaction, and integration (of four language modalities and of language and content) (p. 4). To determine if these principles are reflected in unit design, teachers can ask themselves the following questions:

- Are grammar and vocabulary instruction adequately contextualized within the unit's content?
- Are the texts authentic, and do the tasks allow students to express personal information/opinions?
- Do students have opportunities to revisit content- and language-based concepts at multiple junctures throughout the unit?
- Do students have opportunities to reflect on their work?
- Do students have opportunities to interact meaningfully with each other, as opposed to performing pre-scripted dialogues or answering questions to which they already know or can easily anticipate the answers?
- Do students have the opportunity to read, listen, speak, and write in an integrated fashion?

There are many similarities between WHERETO and CAPRII. For example, the P of CAPRII addresses the same idea as the R of WHERETO: that learning is a process involving systematic revisiting and reviewing of concepts. Any language teacher would agree: there are some structures that take a long time for students to learn, no matter how much concerted effort is expended (Ellis & Shintani, 2014).

Importantly, CAPRII is an excellent fit with a content-based approach to foreign language education. As previously discussed, content provides an authentic context for language learning in CBI, allowing students to speak from their authentic voices rather than putting themselves into hypothetical situations they may never find themselves in, which are numerous in commercial foreign language textbooks. Furthermore, CAPRII compels us to move away from the linguistic syllabus that has dominated foreign language education for so long and produced lackluster results (Martel, 2013).

4.3.2 Example

My unit on (anti)racism in Quebec reflects the WHERETO framework in that I:

- present the unit's essential questions and summative performance task in lesson one (W);
- hook the students' interest using photos of a Black Lives Matter protest in lesson one (H);
- teach the students about the conditional as a resource for expressing intentions for combating racism in lessons two, three, and five (E);
- revisit the unit's essential questions at the end of most lessons (R);
- ask students to discuss how their thinking about discrimination has evolved in lesson four (E);
- ask the students to develop their own questions to ask the guest speaker in lesson eight (T); and
- structure the unit as an "unfolding story or problem" about racism in Quebec (O; McTighe & Wiggins, 2004, p. 225).

Furthermore, the unit reflects the CAPRII framework in that I:

- contextualize the conditional verb form and vocabulary foci into the theme of (anti)racism in Quebec (C);
- use authentic texts throughout the unit, as well as an authentic op-ed summative performance task (A);
- ask students to revisit their thinking about the unit's essential questions at the ends of most lessons and provide them with multiple passes at using the conditional to express their aspirations for action (P);
- have the students reflect at the end of the unit on lingering questions and uncertainties about racism and anti-racist action (R);
- frequently ask the students to engage in meaningful conversations about the content with their classmates (I); and
- ask the students to engage in all three modes of communication: interpretive, interpersonal, and presentational (I).

4.3.3 Your Turn

Look back at the lessons you designed for your thematic unit as a whole. Starting with WHERETO, analyze the lessons using the guiding questions listed above. Based on your answers, make modifications and fill in gaps where necessary. Then, repeat the same process for CAPRII.

4.4 Summary

In this chapter, I explored strategies for designing content and language integrated lesson plans for thematic units. I suggested the following:

- articulating objectives that attend to content and language in a balanced way across the unit;
- constructing lesson plans based on phases, including opening activities, main activities, and closing activities; and
- analyzing the unit as a whole to make sure it reflects principles of effective (language) curriculum design.

Looking forward, I close the book with a few parting thoughts, including a return to the interaction between CBI and our identities as foreign language educators, ways we can use CBI to conceptualize complete foreign language courses, and strategies for using CBI with novice-level learners.

4.5 Reflection Questions

- What does it mean to you for a thematic unit to tell a story?
- What sections/phases are your lessons generally divided into?
- Which routines do you rely on when planning lessons?
- To what extent does your current curriculum reflect the WHERETO framework?
- To what extent does your current curriculum reflect the CAPRII framework?

4.6 Key Resources

- *Understanding by Design: Professional Development Workbook* (McTighe & Wiggins, 2004). This companion guide to Wiggins and McTighe (2005) contains numerous worksheets that help readers understand and implement key backward design concepts.

- *Lesson Planning: Key Concepts and Skills for Teachers* (Savage, 2015). This book addresses the multiple facets of lesson planning to a depth greater than any other resource I know.
- *Scaffolding Language Development in Immersion and Dual Language Classrooms* (Tedick & Lyster, 2020). Destined for dual language and immersion teachers, this book deeply explores the interface between language and content from both instructional and planning angles. The fourth part of the book focuses on curriculum planning and assessment.

Notes

1 In Savage's (2015) model, closing phase activities consist of plenaries, in which the teacher speaks to the whole class collectively.
2 See also the "Interactive Model for Developing Interpretive Communication" in Shrum and Glisan (2016, p. 198).

References

Abrams, Z. (2016). Creating a social context through film: Teaching L2 pragmatics as a locally situated process. *L2 Journal, 8*(3), 23–45.

Brown, H., & Lee, H. (2015). *Teaching by principles: An interactive approach to language pedagogy* (4th ed.). Pearson.

Clementi, D., & Terrill, L. (2013). *The keys to planning for learning: Effective curriculum, unit, and lesson design.* ACTFL.

Curtain, H., & Dahlberg, C. (2016). *Learners and languages: Making the match: World language instruction in K–8 classrooms and beyond* (5th ed.). Pearson.

Egan, K. (1986). *Teaching as story telling: An alternative approach to teaching and curriculum in the elementary school.* University of Chicago Press.

Ellis, R., & Shintani, N. (2014). *Exploring language pedagogy through second language acquisition research.* Routledge. http://dx.doi.org/10.4324/9780203796580

Flowerdew, J., & Miller, L. (2005). *Second language listening: Theory and practice.* Cambridge University Press.

Glisan, E., & Donato, R. (2017). *Enacting the work of language instruction: High-leverage teaching practices.* ACTFL.

Hall, J. K. (2001). *Methods for teaching foreign languages: Creating a community of learners in the classroom.* Pearson.

Lyster, R. (2017). Language-focused instruction in content-based classrooms. In M. Snow & D. Brinton (Eds.), *The content-based classroom: New perspectives on integrating language and content* (pp. 109–123). University of Michigan Press.

Martel, J. (2013). Saying our final goodbyes to the grammatical syllabus: A curricular imperative. *French Review, 86*(6), 1122–1133. http://dx.doi.org/10.1353/tfr.2013.0106

McTighe, J., & Wiggins, G. (2004). *Understanding by design: Professional development workbook*. ASCD.

Paesani, K., Allen, H., & Dupuy, B. (2016). *A multiliteracies framework for collegiate foreign language teaching*. Pearson.

Peregoy, S., & Boyle, O. (2008). *Reading, writing, and learning in ESL: A resource book for teaching K–12 English learners* (2nd ed.). Pearson. http://dx.doi.org/10.5054/tj.2011.244400

Savage, J. (2015). *Lesson planning: Key concepts and skills for teachers*. Routledge. http://dx.doi.org/10.4324/9781315765181

Shrum, J., & Glisan, E. (2016). *Teacher's handbook: Contextualized language instruction* (5th ed.). Cengage.

Tedick, D. (2003). CAPRII: Key concepts to support standards-based and content-based second language instruction. *CoBaLTT Web Resource Center*. https://carla.umn.edu/cobaltt/modules/strategies/CAPRII/READING1/CAPRII.HTM

Tedick, D., & Lyster, R. (2020). *Scaffolding language development in immersion and dual language classrooms*. Routledge. http://dx.doi.org/10.4324/9780429428319

Wayne State University. (n.d.). *S.M.A.R.T. objectives worksheet example*. https://hr.wayne.edu/leads/phase1/smartobjworksheetexample.pdf.

Wiggins, G., & McTighe, J. (2005). *Understanding by design*. Pearson.

Conclusion

In this book, I explored CBI, which is defined as "a curricular and instructional approach in which nonlinguistic content is taught to students through the medium of a language that they are learning as a second, heritage, indigenous, or foreign language" (Tedick & Cammarata, 2012, p. S28). First, I introduced CBI, explained how it has been implemented to date in foreign language education, provided a rationale for expanded adoption, and reflected on how it interfaces with our identities as foreign language teachers. Then, I described strategies for conceptualizing a content-based nucleus for thematic units, which includes essential questions, enduring understandings, and a summative performance assessment. Next, I described strategies for designing learning goals and formative assessment practices that correspond with the content nucleus, with a focus on skills and knowledge development. Finally, I described strategies for designing individual lesson plans, keeping in mind that a thematic unit's lessons build on each other in a logical sequence and prepare students to succeed on the summative performance task.

As a way of concluding the book, I would like to leave you with some parting thoughts on the following topics: (1) identity and agency, (2) course-level planning and alignment, (3) novice-level learners, and (4) a complete unit example.

Identity and Agency

In the first chapter, I invited you to deepen or adopt three facets of your foreign language teacher identity: innovator, curriculum designer, and integrated content and language teacher. I asked you to see yourself as someone who is open to trying new things, who takes an active role in creating their curriculum rather than using a pre-fabricated product,

DOI: 10.4324/9781003017424-6

and who is committed to stimulating student learning in the domains of both content and language.

Having enacted the curriculum design strategies presented in this book, I think it's important to share that I struggle myself at times with these identity aspirations particularly with feeling like I don't know content areas beyond foreign language education well enough to teach them. I know I am not alone in this regard; in a recent study (Martel, 2020), colleagues of mine at the Middlebury Institute of International Studies who implement CBI expressed feelings of discomfort associated with their lack of content expertise. However, I am optimistic that there are ways to mitigate such discomfort. I'll share four ideas here.

First, lean into your identity as a lifelong learner (ACTFL/CAEP, 2013; National Board for Professional Teaching Standards, 2010). I am sure that you like learning new things, since you are reading this book, and you can always expand your knowledge in any subject area, which you can in turn share with your students. Second, seek out collaborations with the goal of learning from others. The participants in my study (Martel, 2020) talked about teaming up with subject-area experts with whom they co-taught content-based courses. Third, remind yourself that all this effort is for a good reason, as research has revealed not only the effectiveness of CBI but also lackluster outcomes associated with traditional approaches to foreign language education. Fourth, lean on your students as sources of content, like the participants in my study did (Martel, 2020). Providing space for students to share what they know about your courses' themes lends authenticity to communication; the students are communicating something you and others truly don't know rather than parroting predictable phrases to practice a pre-selected vocabulary item or grammar point.

I also asked you in the first chapter to exercise your agency as a foreign language teaching professional. I wanted to prime you with this concept because I suspect that you may have to engage in a fair amount of advocacy to get your colleagues to warm up to CBI, especially the content-driven, student-centered iteration outlined in this book. Such advocacy could include sharing and discussing relevant research and inviting those who are interested to watch you teach a lesson from a content-based thematic unit. So far, CBI hasn't truly broken into mainstream foreign language pedagogy; more bottom-up (and potentially top-down) action is needed (Martel, 2013).

Course-Level Planning and Alignment

This book focuses primarily on curricular design strategies for use at the unit and lesson levels. However, Wiggins and McTighe (2005) note that their tools can be used for planning at the course level and beyond. They state:

> What design work at the macro level will render unit design more efficient, coherent, and effective? Our predictable answer: the design of *course* syllabi and *program* frameworks using backward design and the same elements found on the UbD unit template. Specifically, we advocate that programs and courses be conceived and framed in terms of *essential questions, enduring understandings*, key *performance tasks*, and *rubrics*. These overarching elements thus serve as a blueprint for all units and the connections between them.
>
> (pp. 275–276, emphasis in original)

The tools discussed in this book can thus be used to conceptualize full foreign language courses and even programs. Like Wiggins and McTighe (2005), I recommend getting comfortable with unit-level design strategies first before moving to course- and program-level planning. As a reminder, the semester-long course in which my (anti)racism unit figures is titled "Social Issues in Contemporary Quebec" and consists of five units based on needs assessment data collected from students: (1) an introduction to Quebec, (2) (anti)racism in Quebec, (3) immigration in Quebec, (4) healthcare in Quebec, and (5) a synthesis unit. The course is framed with an overarching essential question: How can learning about Quebec help you better understand your work as a policy or management professional? Students' understandings as they relate to this question are assessed at the end of the course during the synthesis unit via an oral performance task in which they present the following information to their classmates:

- an explanation of the nature of the work they will do after graduating;
- an explanation of the reasons for which they chose their field of study;
- an explanation of how our exploration of social issues in contemporary Quebec informs their understanding of their work as policy or management professionals; and
- ways in which they plan to address these and similar issues in their work as policy or management professionals.

Like lessons in thematic units, the thematic units in my course build on each other, preparing students for success on the final unit's summative performance task. Racism is a salient strand, as it is initially explored in the second unit, but resurfaces again in discussions of immigration and healthcare in the third and fourth units, respectively.

If you work in a program that has many sections of the same course, and if standardization across sections is desired or required, you may be wondering how to manage such an approach to course-level planning. Three suggestions come to mind. First, think about standardization primarily through the lens of content, not language. Historically, language courses have been defined by the main grammar points they cover (e.g., the subjunctive in French III) rather than the content-based information and ideas they ask students to explore. This shift involves rethinking course nomenclature, e.g., "Social Issues in Contemporary Quebec" rather than "Intermediate French." Second, decide on a workable level of content-driven standardization for your context, which could take one of many forms:

- course-level content domains are standardized across the program, while the rest is idiosyncratic, based on student needs;
- course-level content domains and thematic units are standardized, while language foci within units are idiosyncratic; or
- course-level content domains, thematic units, and language foci are standardized, with an emphasis on content-obligatory language (Snow, Met, & Genesee, 1989).

Note that there is a key tradeoff among these choices: the more standardized the curriculum, the less likely it is to align with students' needs, meaning potentially diminished engagement and learning.[1] Third, advocate to appropriate stakeholders (e.g., your department chair) for a responsive approach to curriculum design like the one described in this book. As I just mentioned, a localized curriculum is more attuned to students' needs and arguably better for their learning.

I want to acknowledge that time is a factor here. Without doubt, it takes more time to design a fresh content-based curriculum than it does to deliver pre-fabricated lessons from a commercial textbook. However, there are ways to mitigate the time demands, such as creating authentic texts and activities banks that everyone in your department can add to and draw from. You'll also save time by seeking authentic texts that are theme-relevant instead of ones that include multiple repetitions of a specific grammar point, the latter of which is certainly a harder task. I will say that in my experience, designing student-driven, content-based curriculum has not felt like an overwhelming amount of work and is immensely more gratifying than the textbook-centered alternative.

Novice-Level Learners

I have heard many say that CBI is not appropriate for novice-level learners, but I don't think this is true. In fact, research has shown that CBI with beginners is not only doable, but potentially more effective than skills-based instruction. For example, Leaver (1997) found that both beginning- and advanced-level Russian learners made substantial proficiency gains after exposure to a content-based curriculum (summarized in Dupuy, 2000).

Thankfully, there are several strategies that can help make planning for CBI in novice-level courses easier. Let's start with interpretive communication, notably working with authentic texts. Choose materials carefully, based on factors such as length, topic familiarity, text structure, and linguistic complexity (Zyzik & Polio, 2017). Remember, however, that linguistically appropriate texts are not ones "that have the exact grammar and vocabulary that students have learned" but instead ones that "have enough language that students can recognize so they can use these recognizable portions on which to scaffold meaning" (Adair-Hauck, Glisan, & Troyan, 2013, p. 33). Also, use level-appropriate tasks, which could include chronologically ordering events, collaborative reading, etc. (Zyzik & Polio, 2017). Graphic organizers like those available at Regents of the University of Minnesota (n.d.) can be helpful in designing such tasks. In addition, choose texts "that are not text-laden" (Adair-Hauck et al., 2013, p. 26), such as information graphics. Finally, consider scaffolding text interpretation during class time and saving tasks such as vocabulary practice or background reading in students' first language for homework (see also Weyers, 1999 and Maxim, 2002, 2006).

Beyond interpretive communication, it is important to sufficiently scaffold language in the interpersonal and presentational modes with beginning-level learners. This can be done by pre-teaching and modeling pertinent vocabulary and/or sentence frames, in line with Ellis and Shintani's (2014) recommendation to focus more on formulaic language with beginners than on grammar rules. Importantly, language should be highlighted and supported throughout a lesson, even if the forms in question do not relate directly to the lesson's language objective(s). Furthermore, it is helpful to build in moments for students to organize their thoughts before producing language, with techniques like the classic think/pair/share (Gibbons, 2015).

Finally, when considering implementing CBI with beginners, free yourself from worrying too much about grammar and focus more on vocabulary development. This is hard for us to do as foreign language teachers given the grammar-driven manner in which our subject has been historically taught. I am particularly struck by Ellis and Shintani's (2014) comments on the topic:

> No amount of meaningful practice [of grammar structures] will absolve learners from having to progress through developmental sequences. At best, it can only help learners advance along them. One conclusion that might be drawn from this is that practice should not be directed at new structures but rather in helping learners achieve greater accuracy in the use of structures that they have already begun to acquire. It was this reasoning that led Ellis (2002) to suggest that the teaching of grammar should be delayed until 'learners have developed a sufficiently varied lexis to provide a basis for rule extraction' (p. 23). In other words, it might be better to focus on lexis (including formulaic chunks) with beginners.
>
> (p. 111)

This quotation demonstrates that there are likely limits to the effectiveness of our pedagogical interventions when it comes to grammar learning, especially early on. It may thus be more productive to focus on helping your students develop wide-reaching vocabularies.

Complete Unit Example

In Appendix G, I present my complete content-based thematic unit on (anti)racism in Quebec, including its content nucleus, content and language integrated architecture, and nine lesson plans. As a reminder, the unit was designed for graduate-level international policy and management students at the Middlebury Institute of International Studies who were rated at a generalized Intermediate Low proficiency level (ACTFL, 2012). Due to the COVID-19 pandemic, it was delivered fully online. I met with the students synchronously for one hour on Monday, Wednesday, and Friday mornings and asked them to complete asynchronous activities in between synchronous sessions. For the purposes of the unit, I conceive of a "lesson" as the activities completed during a synchronous session plus the activities assigned after it asynchronously for homework, to be completed before the next synchronous session. The unit has been revised since it was initially delivered based on my own critical reflections as well as on feedback from colleagues and students.

I recommend taking time to study the complete unit in depth before pondering this conclusion's reflection questions so that you have more to chew on as you take stock of all that has been discussed.

I have included reflection questions specific to the unit at the end of Appendix G. Furthermore, I realize that it may be challenging for you to envision how to enact such a unit in your own classroom if you teach a language other than French or work with students at a different age or proficiency level. To this end, I have created a website that will serve as a repository for teachers to submit content-based thematic units from a variety of contexts, accessible at http://cbi.middcreate.net/movingbeyond. I plan over time to gather examples for the website from secondary- and university-level teachers across as many languages as possible, as well as videos of enacted lessons. In particular, I hope to include novice-level content-based thematic units. If you are interested in submitting a sample unit, please visit the website for more information.

I see this unit as a living document that will continue to evolve and improve over time, driven by additional opportunities to teach it and reflect on it. In fact, I had a fascinating conversation with friends just two days before submitting the final draft of this book that compelled me to make some non-trivial changes to the summative performance task and seventh lesson plan. I wholeheartedly agree with Nation and Macalister (2010), who state that "[c]urriculum design can be seen as a kind of writing activity and as such it can usefully be studied as a process" (p. 1). I am excited to see the direction the unit will take as I encounter new texts, understand the thematic content better, and learn more from my colleagues and students.

Onward

Thank you very much for taking the time to read this book. I hope that it not only piqued your interest in CBI, but also provided you with tangible curriculum design strategies that you can start using as soon as tomorrow in your language courses. I believe that CBI holds tremendous potential for making foreign language education an even more meaningful and impactful subject than it already is. There is much work to do, however, and I am hoping that we can work together toward that future.

Reflection Questions

- Have you noticed any changes in your identity as a foreign language teacher while reading this book?
- How comfortable would you be advocating for the curriculum design practices described in this book, e.g., to your colleagues or to your boss?

- How can you involve your students in designing your curriculum?
- To what extent might time as a resource shape your ability to implement the strategies described in this book?
- Can you see yourself using this approach to curriculum design with beginning-level students? Why or why not?
- How do you feel about CBI now that you've finished reading this book?

Note

1 I should note that I chose the course theme of social issues in contemporary Quebec, not my students. Enlisting students in choosing course themes would represent an additional level of student-centeredness.

References

ACTFL. (2012). *ACTFL proficiency guidelines 2012*. https://www.actfl.org/resources/actfl-proficiency-guidelines-2012

ACTFL/CAEP. (2013). *ACTFL/CAEP Program standards for the preparation of foreign language teachers*. https://www.actfl.org/sites/default/files/caep/ACTFLCAEPStandards2013_v2015.pdf

Adair-Hauck, B., Glisan, E., & Troyan, F. (2013). *Implementing Integrated Performance Assessment*. ACTFL.

Dupuy, B. (2000). Content-based instruction: Can it help ease the transition from beginning to advanced foreign language classes? *Foreign Language Annals, 33*(2), 205–223.

Ellis, R. (2002). Does form-focused instruction affect the acquisition of implicit knowledge? *Studies in Second Language Acquisition, 24*(2), 223–236. http://dx.doi.org/10.1017/S0272263102002073

Ellis, R., & Shintani, N. (2014). *Exploring language pedagogy through second language acquisition research*. Routledge.

Gibbons, P. (2015). *Scaffolding language, scaffolding learning: Teaching English language learners in the mainstream classroom* (2nd ed.). Heinemann.

Leaver, B. (1997). Content-based instruction in a basic Russian program. In S. Stryker & B. Leaver (Eds.), *Content-based instruction in foreign language education: Models and methods* (pp. 31–55). Georgetown University Press.

Martel, J. (2013). Saying our final goodbyes to the grammatical syllabus: A curricular imperative. *French Review, 86*(6), 1122–1133. http://dx.doi.org/10.1353/tfr.2013.0106

Martel, J. (2020). The identities of language-trained content-based teachers: An underexplored community of practice. *Teacher Learning and Professional Development, 5*(1), 37–48.

Maxim, H. (2002). A study into the feasibility and effects of reading extended authentic discourse in the beginning German language classroom. *Modern Language Journal, 86*(1), 20–35. http://dx.doi.org/10.1111/j.1540-4781.2006.00382.x

Maxim, H. (2006). Integrating textual thinking into the introductory college-level foreign language classroom. *Modern Language Journal*, *90*(1), 19–32.

Nation, I., & Macalister, J. (2010). *Language curriculum design*. Routledge.

National Board for Professional Teaching Standards. (2010). *World languages standards*. https://www.nbpts.org/wp-content/uploads/ECYA-WL.pdf

Regents of the University of Minnesota (n.d.). *Customizable graphic organizer templates.* https://carla.umn.edu/cobaltt/modules/strategies/gorganizers/EDITABLE.HTML

Snow, M., Met, M., & Genesee, F. (1989). A conceptual framework for the integration of language and content instruction. *TESOL Quarterly*, *23*(2), 201–217.

Tedick, D. & Cammarata, L. (2012). Content and language integration in K–12 contexts: Student outcomes, teacher practices, and stakeholder perspectives. *Foreign Language Annals*, *45*(S1), S28–S53. http://dx.doi.org/10.1111/j.1944-9720.2012.01178.x

Weyers, J. (1999). The effect of authentic video on communicative competence. *Modern Language Journal*, *83*(3), 339–349. http://dx.doi.org/10.1111/0026-7902.00026

Wiggins, G., & McTighe, J. (2005). *Understanding by design*. Pearson.

Zyzik, E., & Polio, C. (2017). *Authentic materials myths: Applying second language research to classroom teaching*. University of Michigan Press. http://dx.doi.org/10.3998/mpub.7892433

Appendix A
Thematic Unit Plan Template

Contextual Information
Language
Student Grade/Age
Student Proficiency
    Level

Content Nucleus
Theme
Essential Questions
Enduring
    Understandings
Summative
    Performance
    Task(s) Prompt(s)

Content and Language Integrated Architecture
Skills Goals
Knowledge Goals
Summative
    Performance
    Task(s) Criteria
Formative
    Assessment
    Procedures

Appendix B
Standards by Subject

Subjects	Standards
Dance, Media Arts, Music, Theater, and Visual Arts	National Core Arts Standards, https://www.nationalartsstandards.org/
English Language Arts	Common Core Standards, http://www.corestandards.org/ELA-Literacy/
Health and Physical Education	SHAPE America's National Standards, https://www.shapeamerica.org/standards/health/
Math	Common Core Standards, http://www.corestandards.org/Math/
Science	Next Generation Science Standards, https://www.nextgenscience.org/standards/standards
Social Justice	Teaching Tolerance's Social Justice Standards, https://www.tolerance.org/frameworks/social-justice-standards
Social Studies	College, Career, and Civic Life Framework, https://www.socialstudies.org/standards/c3
Technology	ISTE Standards for Students, https://www.iste.org/standards/for-students

Appendix C
Content Research Planning Guide

Source	Key Resources	Key Information and Ideas
Educational Background		
Interviews with Colleagues		
Other Content Standards (K–12)		
Other Departmental Websites/ Syllabi (Higher Education)		
Authentic Texts (Included in Unit)[a]		
Other Texts (Not Included in Unit)		

a Try to list these texts in a logical sequence of use.

Appendix D

Language Analysis Planning Guide

Source	Functions	Forms
Summative		
Performance		
Task		
Authentic Texts		
Prior Curriculum		
Students		

Appendix E
Lesson Objectives Planning Guide

Lessons	*Objective(s)*
First Lesson	
Second Lesson	
Third Lesson	
Fourth Lesson	
Fifth Lesson	
Sixth Lesson	
Etc.	

Appendix F
Lesson Plan Template

Objective(s)

Procedures
Opening
  Activity(ies)
Main
  Activity(ies)
Closing
  Activity(ies)

Homework

Formative Assessment Findings

Critical Reflections

Appendix G
Complete Unit Example
(Anti)racism in Quebec

Thematic Unit Plan

Contextual Information

Language	French
Student Grade/Age	Graduate
Student Proficiency Level	Intermediate Low

Content Nucleus

Theme	(Anti)racism in Quebec
Essential Questions	• How does racism operate in Quebec?
	• How can racism be combated in Quebec?
Enduring Understandings	• Quebec struggles with racism, even if some say that racism is not a problem in Canada.
	• Combating racism requires persistent effort and engagement in situations that will not always be comfortable.
Summative Performance Task(s) Prompt(s)	As a budding international policy or management professional, you are keeping up with social issues of the day and have turned your attention to Quebec. You have studied how racism operates in the province and want to use this new knowledge to reflect on your own lived experience. Write an op-ed to the Montreal newspaper *Le Devoir* in which you explain how your study of Quebec has shaped your personal aspirations for combating racism at multiple levels in your home community(ies). Your op-ed should be about one single-spaced page in length and contain the following elements:
	• An opening paragraph, in which you state the problem and support it with pertinent information
	• A body paragraph(s), in which you advance personal goals to combat racism
	• A call-to-action paragraph, in which you advance societal goals to combat racism

(Continued)

Content and Language Integrated Architecture

Skills Goals	Students will be able to:
	• interpret and discuss authentic texts related to racism in Quebec
	• define key concepts associated with racism
	• explain cultural perspectives associated with racism in Quebec
	• synthesize information about the state of affairs of racism in Quebec
	• express personal and societal goals for combating racism
Knowledge Goals	Students will know:
	• key concepts like (systemic) racism, whiteness, intersectionality, xenophobia, etc.
	• ways in which systemic racism operates in Quebec
	• important legal tenets regarding policing and race in Quebec
	• key statistics regarding racial profiling in Quebec
	• various methods for combating systemic racism
	• key vocabulary related to (anti)racism in Quebec
	• conjugation rules for the conditional
	• usage rules for the conditional
Summative Performance Task(s) Criteria	• You demonstrate a sophisticated understanding of (anti)racism in Quebec
	• You provide a minimum of two pertinent pieces of information about (anti)racism in Quebec learned from the texts we studied in class
	• You provide a minimum of one new piece of information about (anti)racism in Quebec learned from your own personal research
	• You adhere to accepted genre conventions for op-eds
	• You correctly use a minimum of two new vocabulary words from the class Quizlet
	• You correctly use a minimum of two conditional forms when making suggestions for personal and societal action
Formative Assessment Procedures	• Observations of student content and language performance during class
	• Brief vocabulary quizzes at the end of synchronous sessions
	• Homework activities completed on Canvas

First Lesson Plan

Objective
SWBAT articulate initial perceptions of cultural values associated with racism in Quebec

Procedures

Opening Activities	• Welcome the students to class. Ask them how they are doing and if there is any news they'd like to share with the group.
	• Share the lesson's objective and agenda of activities for the hour.
Main Activities	• Present the unit's essential questions. Check the students' understanding of the questions. Ask them to share why they think it's important to address these questions.
	• Show the students an image of a Black Lives Matter protest from Montreal.[1] Give an example of a descriptive statement about the image using the sentence starter *Dans cette photo, je vois...* (In this photo, I see...).[2] Put the students in groups and have them generate descriptive statements about the photo.[3] Regroup in plenary to go over their statements, providing feedback where necessary (e.g., pointing out statements that go beyond description and venture into inference).
	• Repeat the same process for analysis statements about the photo, using the example sentence starter *Cette manifestation a eu lieu parce que...* (This protest happened because...).
	• Repeat the same process for evaluative statements about the photo, using the example sentence starter *Cette photo me rend XXX parce que...* (This photo makes me feel XXX because...).
Closing Activities	• Explain how the photo exercise we just completed is the beginning of our exploration into the state of racism in Quebec. Give an overview of the main activities we'll complete during the unit, including the summative op-ed performance task.
	• Tell the students that for homework they'll watch a video about racism and systemic discrimination. Ask them to share what they know already about the topics.
	• Explain the homework.

(*Continued*)

Homework[4]
- Study the following vocabulary words on the unit's Quizlet: *taux de chômage* (unemployment rate), *personne racisée* (racialized person), *inégal* (unequal), *embauche* (hires), *défavorise* (puts at a disadvantage), *au sein de* (within), *siègent* (sit on), *issu de* (from).[5]
- Watch the video *Qu'est-ce que le racisme et la discrimination systémiques?* (What are racism and systemic discrimination?; Office de consultation publique de Montréal, 2019). As you watch, try to answer the following questions, which will be discussed during the next synchronous session. You can write down your answers or simply think about them. Rewatch the video as many times as needed and apply subtitles if you'd like.[6]
  - In which practical domains does systemic racism manifest itself?
  - What indicates racism in these domains?
  - What role do institutions play in systemic racism?
  - What is intersectionality?
  - What does the composition of administrative bodies demonstrate about intersectionality?
  - Is there a conceptual difference between the terms *racisé* in French and "people of color" in English?
  - How can inaction reflect racism?
- Add any other vocabulary words from the video that you consider important to the subject matter to the unit's Quizlet.[7]

Second Lesson Plan

Objective
SWBAT define racism and systemic discrimination

Procedures

Opening Activities	• Welcome the students to class. Ask them how they are doing and if there is any news they'd like to share with the group.
	• Share the lesson's objective and agenda of activities for the hour.
Main Activities	• Put the students in groups to discuss their answers to the questions assigned for homework. Regroup in plenary to go over the answers, providing feedback where necessary.
	• Give the students a few minutes to reflect on instances in their own lives during which they've witnessed or experienced racism. Put them in groups to discuss their thoughts. If they're not comfortable doing so, they can listen to and ask questions of their group members. Remind them to express their experiences using the *passé composé* (compound past), e.g., *j'ai témoigné* (I witnessed), *j'ai vécu* (I lived/experienced). Regroup in plenary and ask for volunteers to share what they learned from their partners.

(Continued)

- Display a few sentences that encapsulate your own aspirations for combatting racism, like the ones below. Check the students' understanding of the sentences and explain why you chose them.
  - *Je **voudrais** être un allié pour les gens racisés.* (I would like to be an ally for racialized people.)
  - *J'**aimerais** rechercher des statistiques sur le racisme dans mon domaine professionnel.* (I would like to research statistics about racism in my professional domain.)
- Tell the students that you'll be exploring how to use structures like the ones bolded in these sentences during the unit. Ask them to provide examples of when they've heard or seen this form before.

Closing Activities
- Revisit the unit's essential questions and ask the students to share their preliminary answers.
- Tell the students that for homework they'll watch a video about white privilege. Ask them to share what they know already about the topic.
- Explain the homework.

Homework
- Study the following vocabulary words on the unit's Quizlet: *privilège* (privilege), *transmis* (transmitted), *loties* (fortunate), *collant à* (adhering to), *grandi* (grown up), *obtient* (obtains), *jouit de* (benefits from), *façon* (way), *agissons* (act), *bénéficier* (to benefit from), *en dépit de* (despite).
- Watch the video *Qu'est-ce que le 'privilège blanc'?* (What is "white privilege?"; BBC News Afrique, 2020). As you watch, try to answer the following questions, which will be discussed during the next synchronous session. You can write down your answers or simply think about them. Rewatch the video as many times as needed.
  - Why would white people be unaware of white privilege?
  - What is the main effect of white privilege?
  - Who is affected by white privilege?
  - How do the examples from the United Kingdom and the United States reflect white privilege?
  - How can white privilege be both a heritage and a cause?
  - What will it take to dismantle white privilege?
- Add any other vocabulary words from the video that you consider important to the subject matter to the unit's Quizlet.

Third Lesson Plan

Objectives
- SWBAT define white privilege
- SWBAT explain how to conjugate and use the conditional

(*Continued*)

Procedures

Opening
Activities

- Welcome the students to class. Ask them how they are doing and if there is any news they'd like to share with the group.
- Share the lesson's objectives and agenda of activities for the hour.

Main Activities

- Put the students in groups to discuss their answers to the questions assigned for homework. Regroup in plenary to go over the answers, providing feedback where necessary.
- Give the students a few minutes to reflect on instances in their own lives during which they've witnessed or experienced white privilege. Put them in groups to discuss their thoughts. If they're not comfortable doing so, they can listen to and ask questions of their group members. Remind them to express their experiences using the passé composé, e.g., *j'ai témoigné* (I witnessed), *j'ai vécu* (I lived/experienced). Regroup in plenary and ask for volunteers to share what they learned from their partners.
- Tell the students that you're going to shift to a grammar point that will help them express their thoughts about combating racism, which you'll explore over the course of the unit.
- Give the students a jumbled list of 18 regular verbs conjugated in the conditional accompanied by their subject pronouns, with three verbs per subject pronoun. Put them in groups to generate the conjugation rules based on these examples. Regroup in plenary and ask them to propose what they think the conjugation rule is, confirming or correcting their suggestions. Present high frequency irregular stems.
- Explain basic uses of the conditional, focusing on expressing desires with the verbs *vouloir* (to want) and *aimer* (to like).
- Ask a few students to state personal aspirations for combating racism using the conditional that are related to the video discussed earlier in the lesson. Write their contributions on the virtual whiteboard, providing feedback where necessary. Save these sentences for future use.

Closing
Activities

- Revisit the unit's essential questions and ask the students to share their unfolding answers.
- Tell the students that for homework they'll watch a video about police brutality. Ask them to share what they know already about the topic.
- Explain the homework.

(*Continued*)

Homework
- Study the following vocabulary words on the unit's Quizlet: *traitement* (treatment), *corps* (body), *prédire* (to predict), *quartier* (neighborhood), *lutte* (struggle), *surveillé* (monitored, watched), *profilage* (profiling), *interpellé* (called out/questioned), *harcelé* (harassed), *demeure* (remains).
- Watch the video *Le racisme systémique, c'est quoi?* (What is systemic racism?; Le Devoir, 2020) until minute 3:17. As you watch, try to answer the following questions, which will be discussed during the next synchronous session. You can write down your answers or simply think about them. Rewatch the video as many times as needed and apply the subtitles if you'd like.
  - What is systemic racism?
  - According to the McGill study, what predicts the size of police presence in a neighborhood?
  - What often happens to people of color who venture into Montreal neighborhoods like *Le Plateau*?
  - In cases of police brutality, who does the public tend to sympathize with?
  - Are there social services for victims of police brutality?
  - How often are police officers prosecuted for cases of brutality?
- Add any other vocabulary words from the video that you consider important to the subject matter to the unit's Quizlet.
- Practice conjugating the conditional for 10 minutes on the website http://conjuguemos.com.[8]

Fourth Lesson Plan

Objectives
- SWBAT characterize the state of racism in Quebec and Canada
- SWBAT articulate personal goals for combating racism using the conditional

Procedures

Opening Activities	• Welcome the students to class. Ask them how they are doing and if there is any news they'd like to share with the group.
	• Share the lesson's objectives and agenda of activities for the hour.
Main Activities	• Put the students in groups to discuss their answers to the questions assigned for homework. Regroup in plenary to go over the answers, providing feedback where necessary.
	• Give the students a few minutes to reflect on whether their understanding of systemic racism and discrimination has evolved over the past few lessons. Put them in groups to discuss their thoughts. Model the sentence frame *Avant, j'ai pensé que…, et maintenant, je pense que…* (Before, I thought that…, and now, I think that…). Regroup in plenary and ask for volunteers to share what they learned from their partners.

(Continued)

Closing
Activities

- Tell the students that you're going to shift back to exploring the conditional, which will help them express their thoughts about combating racism.
- Ask for a volunteer to explain how to conjugate and use the conditional.
- Display the sentences that students generated in the previous synchronous session expressing personal aspirations for combating racism. Put the students in groups to add to this preliminary list based on new insights from the video discussed earlier in the lesson. Regroup in plenary and have them share their new ideas. Write their sentences on the virtual whiteboard, providing feedback where necessary.
- Revisit the unit's essential questions and ask the students to share their unfolding answers.
- Briefly quiz the students on a few of the vocabulary words encountered so far in the unit using Quizlet.
- Explain the homework.

Homework
- Submit three new sentences that encapsulate your personal aspirations for combating racism.
- Study the following vocabulary words on the unit's Quizlet: *piste de solution* (pathways to solutions), *enquête* (study), *décès* (death), *impunité* (impunity), *dénonce* (denounce), *inculpé* (accused), *armement* (weapon), *former* (to train).
- Watch the video *Le racisme systémique, c'est quoi?* (What is systemic racism?; Le Devoir, 2020) from minute 3:17 to the end. As you watch, try to answer the following questions, which will be discussed during the next synchronous session. You can write down your answers or simply think about them. Rewatch the video as many times as needed and apply the subtitles if you'd like.
  - Why does the speaker question the independent nature of the CBC study?
  - How many people were killed by the police in Quebec between 2017 and 2019?
  - How many police officers were convicted for these deaths?
  - What do these statistics say about the justice system?
  - How do these statistics compare to other countries?
  - What are two changes to policing the speaker proposes?
- Add any other vocabulary words from the video that you consider important to the subject matter to the unit's Quizlet.

Fifth Lesson Plan

Objectives
- SWBAT summarize strategies for combating racism
- SWBAT explain how to use *devoir* (to have to) in the conditional

(Continued)

Procedures

Opening
Activities

- Welcome the students to class. Ask them how they are doing and if there is any news they'd like to share with the group.
- Share the lesson's objectives and agenda of activities for the hour.

Main Activities

- Put the students in groups to discuss their answers to the questions assigned for homework. Regroup in plenary to go over the answers, providing feedback where necessary.
- Give the students a few minutes to reflect on how they would feel if they were victims of police brutality like the people described in the video. Put them in groups to discuss their thoughts. If they're not comfortable doing so, they can listen to and ask questions of their group members. Remind them that they can use the conditional to express their feelings, e.g., *Je me sentirais XXX parce que...* (I would feel **XXX** because...). Regroup in plenary and ask for volunteers to share what they learned from their partners.
- In plenary, tell the students that you're going to shift back to exploring the conditional, which will help them express their thoughts about combating racism.
- Explain how the verb *devoir* (to have to) is used in the conditional to make suggestions or give advice. Give an example related to combating racism at a societal level, e.g., *Nous devrions communiquer nos valeurs à nos représentants* (We should communicate our values to our elected representatives).
- Ask a few students to state societal aspirations for combating racism using the conditional of *devoir* that are related to the video discussed earlier in the lesson. Write their contributions on the virtual whiteboard, providing feedback where necessary. Save these sentences for future use.

Closing
Activities

- Revisit the unit's essential questions and ask the students to share their unfolding answers.
- Tell the students that for homework they'll read about strategies for confronting racism. Ask them to share what they know already about the topic.
- Explain the homework.

Homework

- Study the following vocabulary words on the unit's Quizlet: *pas* (step), *repérer* (to notice, spot), *pensionnat* (boarding school), *autochtone* (native, indigenous), *contrer* (to counter, block), *se taire* (to be quiet), *témoin* (witness), *se solidaris*er (to unite/show solidarity with), *à l'aise* (comfortable), *contredire* (to contradict), *combler* (to fulfill), *main d'oeuvre* (labor), *réussite* (success), *milieu socio-économique* (socioeconomic status), *lutte* (struggle, conflict), *manifestation* (protest), *atelier* (workshop).

(*Continued*)

- Read pages 11–14 of the document *Petit guide pour combattre le racisme au Québec* (Short guide for combating racism in Quebec; MEPACQ, 2020). As you read, take notes on the following:
  - Three new pieces of information that are interesting to you
  - Two text-to-text, text-to-self, or text-to-world connections[9]
  - One lingering question
- Add any other vocabulary words from the video that you consider important to the subject matter to the unit's Quizlet.

Sixth Lesson Plan

Objectives
- SWBAT summarize strategies for combating racism
- SWBAT articulate societal goals for combating racism using the conditional

Procedures

Opening Activities	• Welcome the students to class. Ask them how they are doing and if there is any news they'd like to share with the group.
	• Share the lesson's objectives and agenda of activities for the hour.
Main Activities	• Put the students in groups to discuss the notes they took for homework. Regroup in plenary to field any lingering questions.
	• Give the students a few minutes to reflect on which strategies from the guide they could see themselves using and what challenges they might encounter in the process. Put them in groups to discuss their thoughts. Remind them that they can use the conditional to highlight their aspirations, e.g., *Je voudrais utiliser cette stratégie parce que…* (I would like to use this strategy because…). Regroup in plenary and ask for volunteers to share what they learned from their partners.
	• Tell the students that you're going to shift back to exploring the conditional, which will help them express their thoughts about combating racism.
	• Ask for a volunteer to explain how to use *devoir* (to have to) in the conditional.
	• Display the sentences that students generated in the previous synchronous session expressing societal aspirations for combating racism. Put the students in groups to add to this preliminary list based on new insights from the guide discussed earlier in the lesson. Regroup in plenary and have them share their new ideas. Write their sentences on the virtual whiteboard, providing feedback where necessary.

(Continued)

Closing Activities	• Revisit the unit's essential questions and ask the students to share their unfolding answers.
	• Briefly quiz the students on a few of the vocabulary words encountered so far in the unit using Quizlet.
	• Explain the homework.

Homework
- Submit three new sentences that encapsulate societal aspirations for combating racism.
- Do research to gather more information about the state of racism in Quebec and strategies for combating it. Seek information that helps you answer the question, is racism a problem in Quebec? Start with the sources listed in the *Petit guide pour combattre le racisme au Québec* (MEPACQ, 2020) and branch out to other sources if you have time, such as recent articles in newspapers like *Le Devoir*.
- Add any other vocabulary words from the video that you consider important to the subject matter to the unit's Quizlet.

Seventh Lesson Plan

Objectives
- SWBAT further characterize the state of racism in Quebec and Canada
- SWBAT articulate similarities and differences between racism in Quebec and in their home countries/regions

Procedures

Opening Activities	• Welcome the students to class. Ask them how they are doing and if there is any news they'd like to share with the group.
	• Share the lesson's objectives and agenda of activities for the hour.
Main Activities	• Put the students in groups to discuss the notes they took for homework and to attempt to answer the question, is racism a problem in Quebec? Regroup in plenary to attempt to come to a group consensus.
	• Tell the students that they are going to reflect on similarities and differences between racism in Quebec and in their home countries/regions. Emphasize that the goal of the activity is to determine whether there are common areas of struggle and/or success. Lead a review of various structures for comparing/contrasting. Highlight conjunctions, using the following example: *Le racisme est un problème au Québec et aux États-Unis* (Racism is a problem in Quebec and the United States).[10]
	• Put the students in groups and give them a digital copy of a Venn Diagram, such as the one accessible at Regents of the University of Minnesota (n.d.). Have them fill in the spaces of the diagram based on the research they conducted for homework and their own personal experiences.

(Continued)

Closing
Activities

Homework

- Regroup in plenary and ask the students to articulate their findings, providing feedback where necessary. Encourage them to engage with each other's statements by agreeing, disagreeing, asking follow-up questions, etc.
- Revisit the unit's essential questions and ask the students to share their unfolding answers.
- Briefly quiz the students on a few of the vocabulary words encountered so far in the unit.
- Explain the homework.

Homework
- Review rules for forming questions at Tex's French Grammar (n.d.), clicking through the various drop-down menus.
- During our next synchronous session, we will have a guest who is a teacher at a community college in Sherbrooke, Quebec. Write five questions you would like to pose to him about the state of racism as he perceives it in Quebec.

Eighth Lesson Plan

Objective
SWBAT request information regarding the state of racism in Quebec

Procedures

Opening
Activities

Main Activities

Closing
Activities

- Welcome the students to class. Ask them how they are doing and if there is any news they'd like to share with the group.
- Share the lesson's objective and agenda of activities for the hour.
- Introduce the guest and explain that he's been invited to share his on-the-ground perceptions of the state of racism in Quebec.
- Lead an open forum during which the students pose questions to the guest and engage in a discussion about racism in Quebec.
- Thank the guest for his willingness to share his experiences and for his time.
- Present the summative performance task to the students, including the rubric and model op-eds from previous students. Field any questions.
- Revisit the unit's essential questions and ask the students to share their unfolding answers.
- Briefly quiz the students on a few of the vocabulary words encountered so far in the unit using Quizlet.
- Explain the homework.

Homework
- Work on the summative performance task. Bring as full a draft as possible to the next synchronous session.

Ninth Lesson Plan

Objective
SWBAT articulate personal and societal goals for combating racism using
the conditional

Procedures

Opening Activities	• Welcome the students to class. Ask them how they are doing and if there is any news they'd like to share with the group.
	• Share the lesson's objective and agenda of activities for the hour.
Main Activities	• Review the rubric for the summative performance task.
	• Using one of the examples shown during the last synchronous session, do a think-aloud evaluation of the op-ed, giving concrete feedback based on the rubric.
	• Put the students into pairs to peer-assess their drafts and ask them to give each other concrete feedback based on the rubric. Repeat the process in new pairs, time permitting.
	• In plenary, ask the students if they have any lingering questions about the performance task.
Closing Activities	• Revisit the unit's essential questions and ask the students to share their unfolding answers.
	• Briefly quiz the students on a few of the vocabulary words encountered so far in the unit.
	• Explain the homework.

Homework
• Finish working on and submit the summative performance task.
• Along with the summative performance task, submit a paragraph in
English in response to the following question: What questions and
uncertainties do you still have about racism and anti-racist action?[11]

Reflection Questions

• To what extent does the unit reflect the design strategies presented
in Chapters 2 through 4? Pay special attention to the following
threads:
   • The ACTFL Standards
   • Content and language integration
   • Critical thinking
   • Social justice
   • WHERETO and CAPRII
   • Inquiry (i.e., students earning knowledge rather than it being
simply told to them)

- Which elements of the sequencing models in Table 4.2 are present in the unit? How are these elements scaffolded across lessons?
- What would you change if you were teaching this unit to students of a different proficiency level?
- What would you change if you were teaching this unit to students of a different age?
- What would you change if you were teaching this unit to students learning a different language?
- Can you see yourself designing and teaching a unit like this? Why or why not?

Notes

1 The photo activity is a DAE (describe, analyze, interpret) exercise, a modification of the classic DIE (describe, interpret, evaluate) exercise from the field of intercultural communication (Nam & Condon, 2010). The purpose of the exercise is to help in

> reversing the usual order of response, withholding one's first reactions, and in the process becoming more aware of how easily and unconsciously one may trespass into the realm of speculation and judgment, and how difficult it can be to limit one's comments to what can be described directly.

> (p. 82)

2 Here, and throughout the unit in similar situations, you could ask the students which other forms/sentence starters they could use to enact the language function in question. This represents an important form of linguistic differentiation (Savage, 2015; Tomlinson, 2014).

3 Whenever the students are in breakout groups, jump from room to room to assist where needed and collect formative assessment data.

4 While these directions are expressed in English here for ease of reading, they should be presented to the students in the target language, accompanied by checks for understanding. This applies to all the lessons in the unit.

5 Previewing key vocabulary is a type of pre-listening/reading/viewing activity described by Glisan and Donato (2017; see also Vandergrift & Goh, 2011 and Hedgcock & Ferris, 2018). I use Quizlet to manage vocabulary learning during the unit. For each word, I include the following information: (1) part of speech, (2) English translation, (3) an example sentence in French using the word, taken from http://wordreference.com, and (4) related words, taken from https://langue-francaise.tv5monde.com/decouvrir/dictionnaire. I aspire to choose words that are content-obligatory (Snow, Met, & Genesee, 1989; Tedick & Lyster, 2020).

6 If text interpretation is impractical or too difficult for your students to do at home, do it during class time instead.

7 I believe that students should have a voice as well as the teacher in determining the focus-worthy words in a text, which is why I give them the opportunity to add their own selections to the Quizlet. Any words students add are viewable by all students.

8 Throughout the unit, I move relatively quickly from explaining how to conjugate/use the conditional to asking the students to use it in free communication. This approach contrasts with commercial foreign language textbooks, which tend to be dominated by controlled practice activities (Aski, 2003 and Fernández, 2011). I hold that authentic (free) communication practice should represent the bulk of a thematic content-based curriculum (see also Ellis & Shintani, 2014).

9 For more information about such connections, as well as a helpful scaffolding document, see Facing History and Ourselves (n.d.).

10 Comparative structures were a grammatical focus in a previous unit and are revisited here to provide further practice.

11 This question is inspired by the list of sentence starters in McTighe and Wiggins (2004, p. 223).

References

BBC News Afrique. (2020, June 21). *Qu'est-ce que le 'privilège blanc'?* BBC. https://www.bbc.com/afrique/monde-53141179

Aski, J. M. (2003). Foreign language textbook activities: Keeping pace with second language acquisition research. *Foreign Language Annals, 36*(1), 57–65.

Ellis, R., & Shintani, N. (2014). *Exploring language pedagogy through second language acquisition research.* Routledge.

Facing History and Ourselves. (n.d.). *Text-to-text, text-to-self, text-to-world handout.* https://www.facinghistory.org/sites/default/files/TexttoText_handout_v.final_.pdf

Fernández, C. (2011). Approaches to grammar instruction in teaching materials: A study in current L2 beginning-level Spanish textbooks. *Hispania, 94*(1), 155–170.

Glisan, E., & Donato, R. (2017). *Enacting the work of language instruction: High-leverage teaching practices.* ACTFL.

Hedgcock, J., & Ferris, D. (2018). *Teaching readers of English: Students, texts, and context* (2nd ed.). Routledge.

Le Devoir. (2020, June 4). *Le racisme systémique, c'est quoi?* [Video]. YouTube. https://www.youtube.com/watch?v=KQBQ-OkCYyA

McTighe, J., & Wiggins, G. (2004). *Understanding by design: Professional development workbook.* ASCD.

MEPACQ. (2020). *Petit guide pour combattre le racisme au Québec.* https://mepacq.qc.ca/tool/petit-guide-pour-combattre-le-racisme-au-quebec/

Nam, K., & Condon, J. (2010). The DIE is cast: The continuing evolution of intercultural communication's favorite classroom exercise. *International Journal of Intercultural Relations, 34*, 81–87.

Office de consultation publique de Montréal. (2019, June 12). *Qu'est-ce que le racisme et la discrimination systémiques?* [Video]. YouTube. https://www.youtube.com/watch?v=S66lC9XbDMU

Regents of the University of Minnesota (n.d.). *Venn diagram.* https://carla.umn.edu/cobaltt/modules/strategies/gorganizers/HGO/20H.PDF

Savage, J. (2015). *Lesson planning: Key concepts and skills for teachers.* Routledge. http://dx.doi.org/10.4324/9781315765181

Snow, M., Met, M., & Genesee, F. (1989). A conceptual framework for the integration of language and content instruction. *TESOL Quarterly, 23*(2), 201–217.

Tedick, D., & Lyster, R. (2020). *Scaffolding language development in immersion and dual language classrooms.* Routledge. http://dx.doi.org/10.4324/9780429428319

Tex's French Grammar. (n.d.). *Introduction to interrogatives.* https://www.laits.utexas.edu/tex/gr/intl.html

Tomlinson, C. (2014). *The differentiated classroom: Responding to the needs of all learners.* ASCD.

Vandergrift, L., & Goh, C. (2011). *Teaching and learning second language listening: Metacognition in action.* Routledge.

Index

Note: Page numbers followed by "n" denote endnotes.

www.ingramcontent.com/pod-product-compliance
Ingram Content Group UK Ltd.
Pitfield, Milton Keynes, MK11 3LW, UK
UKHW020425010325
455677UK00029B/1004